The Connected Peaceful Parent

How to Avoid Being a Toxic
Parent by Connecting with Self and
Mastering Your Emotions to Raise
Happy Kids

Ashley Hardoon

Contents

Get more proactive and less reactive!

Introduction

Perhaps it takes courage to raise children.
John Steinbeck, East of Eden

When was the last time you felt the burnout that accompanies parenting, causing you to criticize or yell at your child? Was it a long time ago? Perhaps not! The good news is that there are things you can do to respond to your child in love instead of with raised voices. How do I know that? Because I have been there. My son and I used to fall into this cycle regularly, but I survived and ensured my son was happy, healthy, and thriving.

According to the 2016 American National Parent Survey, 42 percent of parents can relate to this scenario, not wanting to yell or raise their voice to their child but doing so anyway. Another 35 percent of parents wish they didn't lose their temper quickly. So, you aren't alone if you want to improve your parenting. Still, many people are left wondering how to effectively discipline their children while maintaining an enjoyable relationship with them. The answer may not be as simple as it seems. Intergenerational toxicity plays a big role in how parents are conditioned to raise their children. In other words, we inherit many parental attitudes from our parents and grandparents, many of which do not involve connecting with the children. Past generations usually focused on the adage that children should be seen and not heard, resorting to some of the same tactics that parents find so troubling today, including yelling, name-calling, and even corporal punishment. If you experienced these consequences when you displeased your parents growing up, you might be more likely to repeat the pattern with your child.

This book attempts to help you redefine your parenting paradigm, break free of the toxic intergenerational cycles, and start parenting with love and logic. Busy parents need straightforward, practical tools that are easy to implement immediately to put the family on track to stronger bonds and healthier home life. Modern life has challenges, but every parent can learn how to avoid toxicity in their home with simple steps. Becoming a loving parent capable of raising great kids is nontrivial and will undoubtedly stretch you, but it is worth the time invested. This step-by-step guide will offer the instructions needed to create and maintain your form of effective parenting.

Like many parents, I faced countless difficult days raising my 10-year-old son. He seemed to taunt my authority at every turn, making me more likely to engage in troubling behaviors, like yelling and losing my temper. Finally, I figured out that if I wanted to parent my son in a way that leads to his happiness and ability to thrive while enjoying our time together, I had to do some serious self-work. Starting with developing a deeper self-aware-ness of who I am, I needed a reflection on how my past experiences shaped me, my current triggers, and my re-sponses to difficult everyday situations. As I learned more about my attachments and parenting style, I realized I inherited some toxic traits from my parents, who en-gaged in behaviors similar to those I displayed with my son. I knew how I felt growing up under that type of parenting, and I wanted something different for my little boy. I looked around at friends raising kids and noticed that some did not have the same propensity to yell at their children that I did. I am a Psychology major. But apparently, that background was not enough to handle the parenting challenges. This realization sparked a desire for change, so I turned to the experts to see what I could glean.

Enthusiastically, I took on the challenge of improving my parenting and booked a full schedule of parenting conferences. I would spend weekends learning how to control my reaction to my son's challenging behaviors in a room full of other parents trying their best to learn better parenting. In my spare time between conferences, I listened to the top parenting podcasts that promised to help me stop raising my voice and start making connections. Everything I learned felt revolutionary then and hooked me on the idea of growing closer to my son through better parenting. Finally, I began to sense that I could shift away from the toxic parenting of my childhood, and I was starting to understand just how much my son craved more positive interactions with me. My son was capable of being a well-behaved child and developed even more so into a calmer and happier version of himself as my yelling started to dwindle.

It wasn't long before I realized I needed more than just a weekend-long seminar or an hour-long podcast. I needed real accountability and the help of an expert to dive deep into my psyche and rout out those destructive tendencies that were undermining my chances of developing a thriving relationship with my son. So I started to attend counseling sessions with a professional therapist to dive deeper into the tips and tricks parenting seminars and podcasts taught me. She helped me figure out where I was going wrong and gave me the tools to control my anger and become a mindful parent. Of course, I wished I had those tools sooner, but I was grateful I could change before it was too late. I didn't want my son to grow up with the same intergenerational toxicity I did. The idea for this book was born out of my desire to share what I was learning with the world so that more parents could connect with themselves, master their emotions, and ultimately raise happier kids.

In addition to my experience with parenting seminars and therapy, I also took on the training process to become a licensed therapeutic foster parent through our state. This entailed many training sessions and continuing education credits every few months that taught me the best ways to interact with the children who would come through our home. Between reading books and attending classes, I had a great crash course in more mindful parenting that would encourage my biological and foster children to express themselves healthily without repeating the toxicity that plagued me early in my parenting journey.

As I made the necessary shifts in my parenting strategy, I felt more at peace with myself and my child. My home life began to reflect the more mindful approach I embraced, and things shifted radically. A parent with inner peace who can afford their child enough attention and freedom to make choices is highly likely to raise a happy, thriving child. I still made plenty of mistakes along the way, resulting in setbacks to my new parenting practices. Still, I was on my way to breaking the chains of intergenerational toxicity. My mistakes ultimately shaped my experiences and contributed to my growing expertise and professional learning. I don't want you to go through the same errors I made, so I wrote this book to share what I learned firsthand. I'm far from perfect, but you can still learn from my mistakes on your way to parenting from the inside out.

What you read in this book is based on the parenting experiences of a foster mom. I aim to share factual and scientifically accurate learnings, tested and proven in practice and relatable for everyone. I have practiced those learnings with my kids and many other parents for years. For example, Maggie was one of the parents I came alongside as a mentor when she admitted struggling to connect with her foster daughter. She felt burnt out, and her child would challenge her to the point of anger. More worrisome, Maggie's daughter was starting to mimic Maggie's outbursts, and the two ended up in shouting matches quite frequently. She knew it was time to break from her old patterns but had not realized how toxic her parenting had become. Maggie felt something was amiss and was desperate to make a change before it was too late, and she permanently damaged the bond with her daughter over their daily spats.

She started implementing some of the techniques I included in this book, evaluating her family history, tracing the cycles, and beginning to manage her emotions. As she became more adept at some of these exercises, she noticed that her emotional management also taught her child to soothe herself better. As a result, the two shared more authentic moments of connection than ever before. Fearlessly, Maggie faced her shortcomings as a parent and worked to shore up those areas to unlearn the toxic parenting traits that haunted her just months back. By replacing her unhealthy behaviors with new and more desirable traits, she renewed her commitment to managing her anger and building a relationship with her daughter, who was watching Maggie model more acceptable behaviors. By breaking the cycle of toxic parenting for herself, Maggie is paving the way for a new generation to raise happier and healthier kids.

This book will give you the advantage of my real-world experience as a learner and a teacher. You will have a leg up on creating a positive environment in your home thanks to my years of learning and my process of implementing these anger management techniques explicitly designed to tackle toxic parenting. The book is organized into three sections. The first part focuses on how your family history and intergenerational toxic cycles could impact your parenting style. From there, the second part segues into how you can avoid toxicity through emotional management, and unlearning unhealthy habits. The third and final part teaches self-regulation strategies to help you develop self-care and love for your child while practicing mindful parenting. This book is about you, the parent! The book's central premise is that good parenting starts with you being at peace with yourself. Your child (especially at a younger age) mirrors your behaviors and habits. So, if you wish to have a happy and thriving kid (or kids), start with knowing yourself, your emotions and triggers, and how to manage them. The techniques for managing your anger and embracing a more mindful approach to parenting have been used by countless others to improve the bond with their children. There is something to be learned here for every parent, no matter what sort of home you grew up in. It is more than possible to make a significant change, overhaul your parenting approach, and raise happier, healthier, and more resilient children.

You can expect a quick, informative, and enjoyable read with many tips and tricks to make your parenting life easier! By the time you finish the book, you will have learned the basics and the absolute must-know tips to start parenting with an improved sense of how you are shaping your child's future. The steps included are practical and applicable to every parent, whether or not you were raised with toxic parenting. After you read this book, you will feel better equipped to start parenting from a place of love and logic. As a bonus, you might even see radical transformation in the relationship with your child as you start from a clean slate by parenting from the inside out. Your children will thrive and know just how loved they are when they see you put some simple yet effective behavior management techniques in your home.

Don't delay when it comes to improving your parenting. You want to be prepared next time you face your child's meltdown. You don't like to respond with your usual go-to tactics because they aren't working for you or your child. I hope you enjoy reading this book and become a calmer and more connected parent afterward. If you enjoyed this book, please submit a review to help future readers like yourself and me as a writer! Let's get started!

Chapter One

The Toxic Parent

Don't worry that children never listen to you: worry that they are always watching you.
Robert Fulghum, All I Really Need to Know I Learned in Kindergarten

Many of us have some childhood memories of feeling guilty, anxious, depressed, distrusted, or overlooked by how our parents treated us. Even after decades, the bitter taste of such memories lingers as if the emotional damage left a toxin behind. That is why toxic parenting is so devastating. Dr. Susan Forward used the terms "toxin" and "toxic parenting" for the first time in her best-selling book Toxic Parents: Overcoming Their Hurtful Legacy and Reclaiming Your Life to refer to parents with consistent patterns of harmful behaviors and not just occasional yelling, anger, or other parenting deficiencies.

Most people think only abusive parents are toxic. However, although physically or verbally abusing parents are toxic, it goes way beyond that in sometimes not-so-obvious ways. Any parenting practice or behavior undermining the child's best interests is toxic. The common denominator of all toxic parents is that they don't put their child's needs and interests above their own. The outcome is a child with damaged self-esteem, susceptible to developing behavioral issues and self-destructive attitudes, and ready to continue the cycle of intergenerational toxicity. In this chapter, we'll discuss various types and traits of toxic parents. You might be surprised to learn about the nuanced and subtle forms of toxic parenting and have some eye-opening and perhaps sad reflections about your childhood. Your family history and how you were parented significantly impact how you parent your child. Maybe your parents had some toxic habits and attitudes. This chapter aims to raise your awareness, help you break free of hurtful past experiences and pave the way to a fresh start with your children. Consider this chapter the first step to giving your children a better version of yourself!

Typical traits of a toxic parent

Before we go further, let me explain that the discussions in this chapter focus mainly on more subtle and nuanced forms of toxic parenting. Parents who abuse their children verbally, physically, or even sexually need in-depth and professional treatments that are beyond the scope of this book. Our focus here is on the parents that look normal; they feed their children, keep them safe, take them to sports classes and school events, and are even respected and successful. Nevertheless, they fail to establish a healthy and secure emotional connection with their children. Instead, they make their children feel unloved, worthless, anxious, and depressed.

So, why do so many seemingly normal and reasonable grown-ups become toxic parents? The common trait of all toxic parents is emotional immaturity. What does that mean? Here is an example: the child tells the parent about her feeling, parent discounts the emotion and makes the child feel invalidated. In this example, the parent is emotionally insensitive and shows no empathy. Even the most caring parents might occasionally act insensitively, lose emotional control, or act impulsively. However, if such moments repeatedly happen and create a behavioral pattern, the parent might not even notice them anymore and feel no cringe or regret afterward. That is when a parent becomes toxic.

Emotionally immature parents are not dependable and cannot forge a secure and supportive emotional attachment to their children. The outcome is an emotionally lonely child who feels guilty because they prefer to think it's their fault rather than accepting that their parent is not trustworthy or dependable. Emotional immaturity depicts itself in various forms, creating different types of toxic parents. Here are some of the most common toxic parenting traits:

Self-centered: A toxic parent often places their needs ahead of their child's. They do not stop considering how their actions may impact their child and instead focus only on the outcome for them.

Abusive: Abuse can take many forms, from emotional to verbal, where parents may call their children names, blame them, subject them to the silent treatment, or even gaslight them and make them question their reality. Of course, these types of abuse can also escalate to physical abuse.

Manipulative: Toxic parents want to get what they want, regardless of how it may impact their family or child. They are willing to go to extreme lengths to get what they want, even manipulating their child. This is more than a simple guilt trip, though. It is a pattern of behaviors designed to get the parent what they want, no matter the situation.

Without boundaries: One of the most common symptoms of a toxic parent is a lack of limits with their child. This often applies to other relationships, but it can be prominent in the relationship with their child. Toxic parents tend to wear others down with their desires, so they always get what they want when the other person tires of their drama.

Promoting role reversal: This is where the parent behaves as if the child is the parent. In other words, the parent expects to receive the child's attention, care, and comfort. A typical example of this role reversal is when the parent expects the child to be their confidant for adult issues such as marriage problems. For example, a mother complaining to her daughter about her unhappy marriage and hoping the daughter to comfort her (instead of addressing the issues with her husband or taking counseling or therapy) is a toxic mother.

Emotionally inconsistent: Imagine a father that is either very loving and cheerful or detached and angry, depending on his mood. Such a parent lacks the emotional regulation to make him predictable, consistent, and emotionally dependable. As a result, the children of such a parent experience elusive moments of joy and connection with their dad. However, they can never trust and rely on him since he might often be emotionally absent and disconnected.

Toxic parenting styles

As mentioned earlier in this chapter, our focus is on less apparent forms of toxic parenting. Of course, we all know that an alcoholic or physically abusing parent is toxic. But how about a highly accomplished doctor or lawyer that constantly pushes his (or her) children to be the best at school or become a successful doctor or lawyer just like himself? Or a mother that makes her daughter feel guilty because she wanted to travel with her partner instead of attending the family Christmas dinner? My experience as a foster mom shows that some seemingly normal and well-intentioned parents have more difficulty realizing how toxic they behave. Hence, I think it is relevant for more readers if we discuss some common but subtle forms of toxic parenting that happen daily in countless families and emotionally damage their children without the parents even realizing it. So, putting the abusers, alcoholics, and mentally ill parents aside, here are some of the most common forms of toxic parents:

The emotionally-unstable parents

These parents suffer the most from emotional immaturity. Their moods and feelings drive them; they cannot regulate their impulses or tolerate frustration and stress, are easily upset, and regularly lose emotional balance. Parents are supposed to be role models for their kids. They should model mature, regulated, and stable behaviors. Unfortunately, emotionally-unstable parents do the exact opposite. They cannot even manage themselves, let alone be a role model or help their children navigate their feelings.

The perfectionist parents

These parents are driven, goal-oriented, and pushy. They won't be satisfied with anything but the best. B+ on the school test is not enough for them, and second place in a sports competition is not good in their eyes. They are highly invested in their children's lives and constantly push them to achieve. The problem is that these parents become too judgmental and out of sync with their children. They are more interested in their children's achievements and less in their feelings, preferences, and day-to-day experiences. One of my foster kids kept practicing piano for years because he was afraid to tell his dad that he hated piano. The children of perfectionist parents spent a big part of their childhood and adolescence in various training, tutoring, studying, practicing, etc. They have little time to play, rest, enjoy their childhood, explore the world, and make friends. In their quest for perfection, these parents could become critical of their children. As children grow, they run away from their perfectionist parents or even sabotage their lives to avenge their harsh parents.

The disengaged parent

These parents are emotionally and sometimes physically absent. They do not connect with their children because they are self-involved, narcissistic, and lack the capacity for emotional intimacy. They are indifferent and uninterested in their children and behave as if they do not care about or see them. Imagine a father who always dismisses his young child and spends evenings watching TV or on social media. Parents could become disengaged for various reasons, such as work-related stress, substance abuse, mental health issues, etc. Parents cannot constantly be present for their children but should spend at least some quality time with them. Disengaged parents are regularly (not occasionally) neglectful of their children.

The helicopter parent

Perhaps you've heard of this term before. These parents are hovering over their children's lives like a helicopter. They micro-manage their children's education, social life, career choices, marriage, etc. Their over-controlling and over-protective attitude prevent their children from developing their individuality, exploring the world, making mistakes and learning from them, developing problem-solving skills, and becoming independent and capable grown-ups. These parents have issues with letting go of their control and tend to sabotage their children's independence to keep their position of power.

In 1967, Diana Baumrind (an American clinical and developmental psychologist) published a paper in Genetic Psychology Monographs to present three main parenting styles: authoritarian, permissive, and authoritative. Since then, several other styles, including neglectful parenting, have been proposed. For example, when you ask your child to do something just because "You are the dad (or mom)," you are being authoritarian. The opposite of authoritarian parenting is permissive parenting. Here, the child can choose, and the parent behaves like their best friend. Authoritative parenting is what most psychologists consider to be the sweet spot. It strikes a good balance between setting boundaries and consequences and offering the child a safe and warm environment. For example, you are authoritarian if you set a rule and ask your child to obey it, no questions asked. But if you discuss the same rule with your child, explain why you put it, let your child express their ideas, and be flexible enough to let go of the rule if needed, you are an authoritative parent. Realize that many parents could start the day authoritatively, and as the day passes and their energy dwindles, they become more permissive. In reality, most parents adopt a combination of multiple parenting styles. What matters is the overall ratio over extended periods.

There are two common threads in defining all parenting styles:

1. How responsive are the parents to their child's needs and interests, and

2. How demanding they are regarding the rules and repercussions.

Toxic parents lack responsiveness and compensate by being overly demanding! Let's review the above-mentioned parenting styles in terms of how responsive and demanding they are:

Authoritarian

Authoritarian parents are very self-focused and parent from a place of extreme authority. They believe they always know best and set strict rules, following what they deem acceptable in a child. As a result, communication with their child often goes in one direction only, from parent to child, and never or rarely the other way around. In this parenting style, parents do not take much time to consider their children's emotional or social needs. It is a high-demand parenting style with little responsiveness to the child.

Authoritative

Most experts agree that authoritative parents are the most likely to pass on good parenting traits to their children. While they still set rules and expectations similar to the authoritarian parent, they are not as strict and often allow natural consequences. This parenting style is marked by open communication with the child and a dynamic relationship that takes problem-solving into account. It makes demands of a child but meets them with a high degree of responsiveness that considers the child's emotional needs.

Permissive

Unlike authoritarian parents, permissive parents are highly child-focused. Permissive parents want to be viewed in a favorable light by their children. As a result, they frequently avoid giving their child any rules or consequences. The goal is to prevent conflict, making the child free to do as they please with little or no instruction, guidance, or boundaries. While permissive parents tend to be highly responsive to their children, they make few demands and set few boundaries.

Uninvolved

Uninvolved parenting, aka neglectful parenting, can be equally harmful to a developing child. In this parenting style, the parent is primarily hands-off with their child and is mostly absent from the critical moments of a child's life. If nurture is essential to a child's development, they may suffer at the hands of an uninvolved parent who provides little nurturing or guidance. An uninvolved parent may know their child's emotional needs but is indifferent to how these can shape a child. As a result, they make few demands of their child and do not respond when their child needs them.

While there can be good things about almost all of these parenting styles, there are certain pitfalls that you may be prone to pass on to future generations. However, just like you can pass along bad parenting styles, you can also pass along an excellent example of an engaged and responsive parent with an authoritative style. That is why knowing your dominant parenting style is essential to take the proper steps toward better parenting.

Do I have toxicity in my parenting?

Most parents do their best to raise happy and healthy children. Nevertheless, they occasionally make mistakes, emotionally hurt their children, and cause them guilt, fear, anxiety, insecurity, or even hate. Imagine your words and actions as drops of water and your child's mind and feelings as a piece of rock. Every damaging word and action pierces their mind drop by drop. A few occasional droplets are no big deal. But a continuous stream of mistakes leaves a permanent scar. Reading this chapter, you might recognize some toxic traits in your parenting. Until now, maybe you did not notice those traits or consider yourself a well-intentioned parent. A vital step to becoming a better parent is to spot your toxic parenting traits and eliminate them before permanent damage is done. In this section, we'll try to dissect your parenting habits and search for signs of toxicity.

Does any of the following statements apply to you?

- You expect everyone to agree with you about everything. Everything is about you and your feelings.

- You don't believe in privacy or independence for your child.

- You are more judgmental of your children than you are of the children of your friends or family members.

- The expectation is that your child will follow in your footsteps or that you can live vicariously through them as they live out your dreams.

- You feel uncomfortable with your child's happiness and do not allow them to express their feelings.

- You use guilt trips consistently to get your way.

- You think your child should make you happy.

- You are afraid of your child's independence.

- You constantly compare your child to others.

- You withhold love and affection as punishment, including silent treatment.

- You take no blame and do not apologize for your actions when things go awry.

- You are overly critical and may make excessive jokes about your child.

- You compete with your child or envy them.

- You micro-manage your child's life and co-opt their goals.

- You believe in tough love and think you can spoil your child with too much love and positive affirmation.

- You do not encourage or even allow your child

to express negative emotions.

- Instead of supporting your child when they need you, you tend to blame them.

- You fail to regulate your emotions toward them, predominantly negative emotions such as anger and frustration.

- You tend to be negative, pessimistic, and killjoy instead of positive, hopeful, and pleasant.

- Instead of modeling good habits, you overly criticize yourself in front of your child.

If any of these statements apply to you, your parenting has some traces of toxicity. If several of them are true for you, you have some serious work to combat your toxic parenting!

For many of us, these traits will apply at one point or another. Truly toxic parents will likely find that they meet many of these criteria and can see a clear pattern of such behaviors. In my time as a foster parent, I saw these toxic traits play out in the biological parents of several of my children. As our foster children grew older and started to have children of their own, we noticed that some were repeating the pattern despite how detrimental it had been to them growing up. If you think and feel you might have some toxicity in your parenting, know that changing course and implementing healthier strategies is more than possible with time and effort. It won't be an overnight transformation, but it can slowly and surely happen. Hopefully, this book will be your companion in this transformation!

Among the statements mentioned above, the last three items are solely about you (and not your parent-child relationship). Parenting starts with you! If you are not at peace with yourself and cannot regulate your emotions, it will be tough (if not impossible) to model good behaviors for your child. Therefore, this book focuses more on you (the parent) than your child. After understating the toxic intergenerational cycles in Chapter 2, we'll discover how to unlearn toxic parenting habits (Chapter 3), emotional regulation (Chapter 4), knowing your parenting personality (Chapter 5), and how to stay attuned to your child in the final chapter.

Negative parent-child interactions set the child up for future interactions with others fraught with challenges. We could see these effects even in young children placed with us, away from their toxic parents. Years of this ingrained behavior resulted in a pattern we saw repeatedly play out in our home. How you were parented plays a significant role in how you parent your child, and to understand why you might show signs of toxic parenting, you need to examine your family history and how your parents raised you. In the last part of this chapter, we'll discuss some typical signs you had toxic parents.

Did toxic parents raise you?

Maybe you could not tell if your parents were toxic as a child. But looking back, now you can objectively look at your parents and their habits. This could be a painful exercise for many of us. But it is an essential step to breaking the intergenerational toxicity cycle. So, what does it look like to be raised by a toxic parent? At a fundamental level, the children of a toxic parent are confused about love. Our parents are the first to love us; we look up to them as our role models and protectors. One can describe a toxic parent with one or more of the following traits: selfish, intrusive, abusive, over-critical, manipulative, unsupportive, and disengaged. The children of such parents will be confused about feeling loved because they do not feel protected and supported by their parents. Eventually, the child grows to connect those unpleasant feelings with being loved and develops trust issues.

Being raised by a toxic parent often results in difficulty developing trusting relationships with others, including friendships and romantic relationships. You may shy away from these relationships even when someone has been kind and honest with you. This was the biggest indicator of toxic parenting in our foster children. One ten-year-old boy could not accept that we would reward him for good behavior, lavish gifts at Christmas time, or tell him the truth when he asked questions. He was used to a toxic mother who always took away her affection when he did something wrong, prompting him to always feel on the verge of losing us and our affection when he inevitably made a mistake, whether at school or home.

Rejection and failure are other aspects of being raised by a toxic parent that might hit you hard. Toxicity and abuse lead most people to struggle with appropriate emotional responses, particularly regarding failure or rejection. For example, if you feel that you have ruined everything or are filled with incomprehensible shame following a failure, it may result from the toxic parenting you grew up with. This is quite common with high-achieving, successful parents. In their pursuit of excellence, and maybe even with good intentions, they don't allow their children to make mistakes and fail. The children of such parents never learn to accept failure as a normal part of their lives. Fearing failure, they do not even try new endeavors; even if they occasionally try, they are likely to blame themselves if they falter.

Because being raised by a toxic parent often means they were overly critical of you as a child and teenager, the odds are that the voice in your head is equally problematic for your self-esteem. As a result, you may be overly critical of yourself, your actions, and your overall achievements. Suppose you were raised with a toxic parent who tended to be hypercritical (bordering on emotional or verbal abuse). In that case, it is only natural that you may have internalized their voice and now deal with this harsh inner critic no matter what may be going right or wrong in your life.

Another symptom of being raised by toxic parents is the tendency to put your emotional needs last or to feel completely out of touch with your own emotional needs.

Toxic parents who prioritize their own emotions above those of their children teach their children that their feelings must take a backseat if they want to avoid conflict and drama. This translates into adults who struggle to prioritize their feelings with a partner or completely shut down with their child. They may not even know their emotional needs because they have spent their formative years catering to emotional outbursts and turbulences with their parents. Any display of emotional vulnerability may be looked down on as harmful if you can experience this "weakness" at all.

If toxic parents raised you, you might have difficulty communicating with them even though you no longer live with them and logically know you are not responsible for their feelings. You may still be afraid of them, whether of their abuse or overly-critical eye. Growing up feeling responsible for their happiness may make you less likely to turn to them in your time of need, even if you are an adult. It is normal to embody some of these traits you despised in your parents growing up, but you should know that breaking the cycle of intergenerational toxicity is possible.

We all fall along the narcissism spectrum; approximately half a percent of the population in the United States suffers from extreme forms of narcissistic personality disorder. Narcissism is also a common trait of toxic parents. If you were raised with narcissism, there is a good chance that it may have impacted you on a deep level. There are two routes you might take if exposed to narcissism in your parents: you might become a narcissistic parent yourself or constantly question your own decisions as a parent. Much like other intergenerational toxic cycles, narcissism can be passed on from parent to child, making it difficult to dig your way out and set a new course for future generations.

Narcissistic traits do not necessarily mean someone has or will develop a narcissistic personality disorder. However, you can see that there is quite a bit of overlap regarding the traits inherent to toxic parenting. For example, narcissistic parents are more likely to verbally or emotionally abuse their children and the other people in their lives. Unlike many toxic parenting traits that apply only to the parent-child relationship, narcissism tends to impact all relationships in a person's life. A narcissist tends to have an extreme sense of entitlement and always puts their needs ahead of those of other family members, including their child. They may move to exploit their children or partner to get their needs met.

A real-life example is a parent who guilts their child into performing the chores that should rightfully belong to the parent, such as making the parent breakfast before school or doing all the housework. Other traits of narcissistic parents can include triangulation, gaslighting, frequent use of silent treatment, blaming or scapegoating, and passive aggression toward the people in their life, up to and including their child. All these behaviors confuse the child and distort their sense of reality.

Unfortunately, these traits can also be passed down from parent to child. Being raised by a narcissistic parent may tarnish your idea of what is healthy and appropriate in a parental relationship. If you grew up thinking it was normal for you to meet the emotional needs of your parent, then you may have difficulty adjusting your expectations when you have a child of your own. Children of narcissists internalize the family value system that places the most emphasis on the parent and teaches that love is conditional. This sets the stage for you to view your child as an extension of yourself; when they succeed, you succeed. When they fail (and it is a certainty that they eventually will), you also view this as an extension of yourself.

Most of my foster kids struggle to speak up about their early childhood memories. But when they occasionally open up, they say something along these lines:

"My parents did not hear me. Sometimes I thought they could not see me."

"They did not like me to hang out with my friends. I could not invite my friends to come over either."

"I was never good enough for them. All they did was blame and criticize me."

"My mom used to shame me in front of her friends."

"My dad used to say everything should be his way."

Maybe the most apparent indicator of whether toxic parents raised you is if you (generally speaking) liked or dreaded going home. Unfortunately, home was a dreaded place for many of my foster kids, and it is a constant struggle for me as a foster parent to change their perception of a home. Once you realize that your parents had some toxic traits and you might have inherited some of them, you can start to make a notable change and break the cycle. This chapter introduced toxic parenting. The next chapter will explain how even well-intentioned parents could turn toxic.

Chapter Two

The Making of a Toxic Parent

The family, that dear octopus from whose tentacles we never quite escape, nor, in our inmost hearts, ever quite wish to.

Dodie Smith, Dear Octopus

Why do parents become toxic? Are they born with toxicity, or do they turn toxic? Where does the toxin come from? Why do we repeat the same behaviors we despised in our parents? You might have thought about these questions on many occasions and even have some answers. One of the most challenging aspects of parenting is that the implications of the parent-child relationship mostly show up with delay (sometimes many years later). That's why toxic parents leave a legacy behind that shows up decades later; a new generation of toxic parents!

This chapter explains how your family history and the parenting style you grew up with form you as a person and a parent. Then, we will discuss intergenerational cycles and trauma and shed some light on why we tend to recreate our hurtful childhood experiences. Can we break the vicious cycle of intergenerational trauma? You'll find that out too in this chapter!

Toxic Intergenerational Cycles

When a child is born, parents are born too. Unfortunately, the vast majority of new parents lack parenting knowledge and (obviously) experience. Unless they educate themselves and practice good parenting actively, almost all new parents fall back on what they experienced in their formative years. In other words, they tend to repeat the habits and behaviors of their parents. When they repeat the negative patterns or traits passed down from their parents, they become a part of the toxic intergenerational cycle.

As a therapeutic foster parent, I saw firsthand how toxic intergenerational cycles played out in real life. One of my foster daughters, a teenager at the time, came from a background of physical and verbal abuse in her biological family. We kept in touch even after she left our home. When she became pregnant at seventeen and started raising her infant son, we noticed that she gravitated toward men much like her biological father. They were loud and abusive, but it took her some time to realize that this wasn't the environment where she wanted to raise her new baby. She didn't want to repeat her parents' mistakes, who had stayed together longer than they should have for the children's sake. It was clear that she was imitating the family life she had when growing up. Not surprising since behaviors are hereditary and passed down through generations. Our foster daughter committed to being the one to break the cycle of toxic parenting. Still, she needed substantial help from us and a lot of counseling to take a different approach with her son.

Toxic parenting starts with the power dynamics of the family. Parents hold all the power, and their children have no voice or freedom to choose. As a result, toxic parents often embrace common myths about their children, even without consciously knowing it. For example, two of the most common myths are that children should be seen and not heard and should always do as they're told. At first glance, these myths seem like excellent benchmarks for parents to determine how well their children are doing. After all, a compliant child who obeys their parents and doesn't make much noise can be a pleasant experience. However, these and other myths can lead to toxic parenting practices at the cost of the happiness and autonomy of the child.

One way we pass toxic behaviors onto our children is by invalidating their feelings. It can be tempting to tell your child to "man up," stop crying, or not to worry about something bothering them. However, this sets the stage for your child to do their best to cover their feelings in your presence. They learn it is more beneficial to put on a façade of happiness and not to upset their parent. Similarly, praising only achievements can have a closely-related effect. A child will learn that achievement is the only valuable thing to be gained from any experience, whether scoring the highest on a math test or scoring the winning goal at a soccer game. Instead, parents must teach their children that all emotions are valid and that achievement is just one small piece of the success puzzle.

Parents who missed out on opportunities in their childhood or even as adults may try to rectify that situation by encouraging their children to pursue specific goals. At first glance, it can seem like a good thing that parents are encouraging their children to be successful. However, if it is taken too far, children can grow to resent their parents for pushing them to experience and participate in life in a way that feels inauthentic and undesired. In addition, parents may create a situation where children are more dependent on them to help guide their decision-making process because they desperately want to please their parents. They may be afraid that their parents will use a guilt trip or fear to get them to comply with their wishes. Therefore, don't set the bar too high for your child to achieve your favor.

Parents can also pass toxic behaviors onto their children by doing everything they can to be their favorite person. While it is normal and healthy to want a child to have a bond with their parents, too many attempts to curry favor can backfire and cause long-term problems for the child later in life. They may turn to the same manipulative tactics used by the toxic parent to try to gain favor from others. It is best to draw healthy boundaries and allow the parent-child relationship to form, even if the parent may not be the favorite. This is something that I saw play out often with the biological parents of our foster children. In an attempt to be the favorite in what they perceived to be a competition with us as the foster parents, they often went out of their way to get their children to like them. This might be buying them expensive presents they couldn't truly afford or agreeing with the child on everything, even when it would have been wiser to set healthy boundaries and enforce them with the child.

Experts believe four critical types of behavior may present in parenting due to toxic intergenerational cycles. Those four behaviors include emotional parentification, parental projection, emotional offloading, and enmeshment. So let's take a closer look at each one:

Emotional Parentification

Emotional parentification is a long term with a pretty simple meaning: parents rely on their children to meet their emotional needs instead of through relationships with other adults or therapy to resolve childhood issues. If parents depend on their children to manage their emotions or seek attention and validation from their children, they are giving into this type of toxic parenting. The bottom line is that your child should not be your confidante or responsible for your emotional well-being! When this happens, you engage in toxic parenting even if you don't realize it.

Parental Projection

When was the last time you projected your feelings onto your child? Maybe you wanted them to make a particular decision because it eased your anxieties or fears about their future. Perhaps you worry if your child will succeed. While some of this worry is typical of any parent, some toxic parents take it too far. They trap their children beneath the weight of their expectations, making it impossible for the child to make their own decisions. Trying to live vicariously through your children signifies parental projection and is a typical form of toxic parenting.

Emotional Offloading

If you emotionally offload, you have difficulty regulating and processing your feelings. Instead, you may dump your emotions on your children, act out toward them, or instigate drama in your home. One sign that you may be emotionally offloading is that you become enraged by little things. You may even become defensive if your child says their relationship with you doesn't meet their expectations.

Enmeshment

Do you struggle to set boundaries with your child in big or small ways? Parents who have no limits with the people in their lives often become codependent or enmeshed with their children. They have no real indication that they are a unique and separate person apart from their family and friends, even apart from their children. Setting boundaries feels like a threat to who they are as a person. Enmeshment often leads to familial drama, mainly when the child is old enough to express their thoughts and beliefs and demonstrate autonomy.

Does any of these issues sound familiar to you? You aren't alone if they do; you aren't alone if you feel like you may fall into multiple categories. Many parents might see reflections of themselves in several of these issues, but the good news is that breaking the pattern of toxic intergenerational cycles is more than possible. You can be the catalyst that breaks the chain and sets your child up to thrive in the years and decades ahead as they start to form their own family.

Intergenerational trauma

Toxic intergenerational cycles create intergenerational trauma. It doesn't take much imagination to explain intergenerational trauma, but you may not be aware of its implications for your parenting. This term refers to trauma that is passed down from one generation to the next, but it may not be as apparent as you imagine. Even if you weren't physically abused as a child, intergenerational trauma could be insidious, influencing your parenting in ways you don't expect as a silent partner in the trenches with you. It can appear in your choices and the words you use to parent your child.

The symptoms of intergenerational trauma are closely related to those associated with post-traumatic stress disorder. Here are some examples:

- Hypervigilance

- Mistrust of others

- High anxiety or panic attacks

- Mood issues like depression

- Nightmares or insomnia

- More sensitive fight or flee response

- Lower self-esteem

- Feeling guilty when happy

Imagine your great-grandfather imposed harsh discipline on his children and did not care much about their feelings. Your grandmother learned to cope with such a father by cutting off her emotions or keeping them to herself. Because of her childhood experiences, she interacted in a distant, unengaged, defensive way with your parents and even with you. This transmission of unresolved negative past experiences over generations is intergenerational trauma. The word "unresolved" is critical here. Not all negative experiences are necessarily passed down. However, if the affected individual examines the traumatic experience, interprets it differently, and resolves it consciously, the trauma won't be transmitted to the next generation. Take the example of Maya Angelou, the great American poet, author, actor, and activist. Her parents divorced when she was three, she was sexually abused at age eight, had a son when she was sixteen, tangled with drugs and prostitution, and yet managed to be one of the greatest poets of modern America and an inspiration for countless people around the world. Maya digested all those negative experiences and decoupled her self-worth from them. She not only didn't pass her traumas along but became a symbol of hope and wisdom for many. We'll talk more about resolving past traumas in the next chapter.

The concept of intergenerational trauma was pioneered in the 1960s by psychiatrist Professor Vivian M. Rakoff, former chair of the University of Toronto's Department of Psychiatry. He examined the psychiatric care referrals of the children of the Holocaust survivors and showed their higher likelihood of psychiatric illnesses. In a 1988 study, Rakoff focused on the grandchildren of Holocaust survivors and found that they were overrepresented by approximately 300 percent when it came to psychiatric care referrals. Even though the grandchildren were far removed from the trauma of the war, the effects of the extreme situations their grandparents experienced had severe psychological implications for them.

It isn't just Holocaust survivors who passed their trauma down to later generations. Trauma can make the next generation more susceptible to repeating the patterns and experiencing psychological distress. This can include physical abuse, exploitation, racism, and even poverty. Certain groups will be at a greater risk of passing intergenerational trauma down to their children, for example, those who are othered because of their skin color or those who have grown up in war zones or are affected by natural disasters such as hurricanes or tsunamis. Even one-time instances such as hate crimes can impact the next generation.

One of my foster sons came from a home where his parents loved him immensely but were constantly at odds with each other. While they had divorced when he was a teenager, they spent his formative years bickering and openly showing their hostility for one another, including in front of their son. They had short tempers with one another and often resorted to name-calling and yelling. Even though neither parent frequently raised their voice to their son, their disagreements and fights harmed him. When he came to us, it was from the local pediatric psychiatry unit where he had been admitted for depression following their divorce. He presented with anxiety and seemed uncertain about how to relate to us as his foster parents when we did not embrace the chaotic lifestyle he had grown accustomed to with his biological parents. He showed the symptoms of intergenerational trauma and needed therapy and self-awareness.

Domestic violence between the parents, infidelity, alcoholism or substance abuse, and even issues like anxiety can lead to intergenerational trauma. In addition, some parents who aren't sure of themselves or confident in their parenting may become anxious and riddled with worry that they aren't providing everything their child needs to thrive. This uncertainty is another intergenerational trauma that can be passed down to children unless the parents are aware of their thoughts and feelings and actively work to combat the anxiety surrounding parenting.

Trauma and Parenting Style

Adversity in childhood often leads to stress for the next generation. Numerous studies point out that parents with severe trauma or stress are far more likely to report high levels of aggravation with their children, and the children are more likely to have mental health problems. Could it possibly be that their approach to parenting leads to increased behavioral problems in their children? Researchers would argue that it does and advocate for pediatricians to take a more well-rounded approach to address intergenerational trauma with parents during a child's wellness visits. Childhood trauma can impact your parenting approach. It may lead to one of the following parenting styles: avoidance, sheltering your child, controlling your child, or neglecting your child's emotional needs. Let's review each style in more detail.

Avoidance

Parental avoidance can take many forms; for example, parents may avoid emotional reactions from their child or activities that trigger the memory of their trauma. However, they may use other coping strategies if the feelings are too strong. Alcohol and drugs are common in parents struggling with avoidance. Unfortunately, an avoidant parenting style leads to even more intergenerational trauma for the children.

Sheltering

Are you eager to keep your child from experiencing the negativity you endured? Unfortunately, parents who try to keep their children safe often swing the pendulum in the opposite direction and shelter their children from experiencing anything negative. This hurts children's autonomy and limits their ability to practice independent decision-making. While it is born out of a desire to protect and shield children, it can ultimately lead to fewer opportunities to explore what interests them because their parent is concerned about them experiencing the same or similar trauma.

Controlling

How often have you seen a Hollywood movie depicting a rebellious teen who grew up under strict parents? This is a common trope for films but has a solid reality-based truth. Parents who experience trauma are eager to establish control over their children, making it less likely that the child will go through the same negative experiences. It is a way for parents as trauma survivors to assert their independence and control over what happens in their lives. However, seeking to control every aspect of your child's life often leads them to rebel, fail to develop independence, and may lead to an inability to handle their emotions.

Neglecting Feelings

Children have emotional needs. Unfortunately, it is common for parents who endured trauma to separate themselves from their children, including holding their children at arm's length and neglecting their emotional needs. Instead, parents should resolve their traumatic experiences to connect emotionally with their children. Unfortunately, the consequences of not doing so are tremendous: children may be unable to handle vulnerability in others or learn to process their feelings independently.

Vehicles of intergenerational trauma

You probably remember your high school biology class; you inherit traits from your parents through the genes that they pass on to you. We get one copy of genes from our mother and one from our father. Together, they combine to form the DNA of our cells. As a result, heredity determines whether you are male or female, your hair color, and how tall you grow up. We often think of heredity in terms of our inherited physical traits, but it goes beyond physical characteristics. We also inherit behaviors and emotions, especially from our childhood experiences. But how does this intergenerational transmission of personal traits occur? And is there such a thing as hereditary parenting behaviors?

The answer may be a little more complex than it seems. There are no straightforward answers regarding how we learn to parent future generations. Some people argue in favor of nature, stating that our genetics determine how we will respond. Others vote in favor of nurture, saying that our future actions are learned from past experiences. It comes down to a classic debate about whether our genetic code or environment is the more prevalent force in shaping us. There may be a role for both of these schools of thought.

In favor of nature, the proteins formed by your DNA create you to be the unique person you grew up to be and affect your behavior. On the nurture side, your environment determines how those proteins and behaviors will be shaped. Scientists who argue that nurture plays the most prominent role in our overall actions believe that certain events may turn our genes on, making it more likely to exhibit a specific behavior. For example, you may be genetically predisposed to having a temper due to the proteins in your genetic code. However, you may only learn to express that anger if you see that behavior modeled by the people around you (especially your parents and other caretakers). Whether or not these genes become activated is the subject of a new field of science known as Epigenetics.

Epigenetics studies the environmentally-driven processes that turn the genes on and off. Of course, your DNA will never change. From the moment you are born, you are stuck with the genetic lottery you won as a fetus in the womb. However, many scientists believe epigenetic mechanisms determine whether certain genes become active or remain dormant in specific contexts. An example of such epigenetic mechanisms is DNA methylation, the attachment of methyl groups (chemical compounds made of one carbon atom and three hydrogen atoms) to DNA building blocks. Our cells use methylation as a common epigenetic signaling tool to turn specific genes off. Scientists believe a sufficiently-high methylation rate plays a crucial role in repressing certain gene expressions (i.e., locking them in the "Off" position). Recent studies by the Icahn School of Medicine at Mount Sinai in New York have shown that children of Holocaust survivors with Post Traumatic Stress Disorder (PTSD) have lower rates of methylation in stress and depression-related receptors and genes than children of survivors who did not have PTSD.

This does signal something vital for us as parents. If you inherited these behaviors from your parents through your genome or the epigenome, you might pass the same traits down to your child. What if you could change the epigenome of your child to make it less likely that they will turn to anger, yelling, and corporal punishment in the future? Would it be worth making a radical change for future generations?

Know your family history!

When expectations are unmet, many parents respond to their children angrily, where the toxic parenting cycle begins. You may turn to spank and other corporal punishment or yell and berate your child. Either way, you likely respond to your child in the same way your parents responded to you in similar circumstances growing up. This is why knowing your personality traits (we'll discuss this in Chapter 5) and family history is crucial; it helps you see where you might fall short in your parenting journey. Once you recognize the patterns in your behavior and how similar it is to the approach taken by your parents, your journey to break toxic intergenerational cycles begins.

If you had a childhood similar to mine, chances are that you had to complete a family tree project during elementary school. For many people, this is the most in-depth they ever go into their family history despite how important it proves for the rest of their lives. Unfortunately, I saw little purpose in pursuing the finer details of my family history until I was deep in the throes of course-correcting with my parenting. Yet, it turns out that understanding your family history is vital to giving you a sense of identity, connection, and more.

When most people think of their family history, they immediately imagine sitting at a doctor's office. At the same time, they try to fill out endless reams of paperwork about which parent had diabetes, which grandparent suffered a stroke, and whether your uncle had any mental health concerns. Medical history is crucial to your overall well-being and can tell much about whether you have a genetic risk for certain conditions. However, your medical history isn't the only thing you should be concerned about. We can inherit cultural and relational issues too. So, knowing what you are against as you take on parenting your child is vital.

How can understanding your family history make you a better parent? First and foremost, knowing where you came from affords you a sense of personal identity. It lets you dive deep into your culture and what separates your family. As a result, you may notice that you are more confident in who you are and have an increased sense of self-worth. Second, uncovering family history can be a great bonding project for you and your child, allowing you to share your self-worth with your son or daughter. Both of you can learn who you came from and where you come from culturally. Finally, it will connect you further with your ancestors and extended family members who may be eager to share their stories.

Once you have done a self-inventory of your personality traits, you can start thinking about how those traits may apply to your parents, grandparents, and other adults who influenced your life. Knowing your family history has tangible benefits for you as a parent and your child. For example, a study at Emory University in 2010 found that children with a great understanding of their family histories experienced improved self-esteem and greater well-being. In addition, they were more likely to report that their family functioned successfully.

Knowing your family history better might make you more compassionate. You will clearly understand where you came from, what made you who you are today, and how that affects your parenting. In my experience as a foster parent, this ability to look compassionately upon your own family is crucial to helping you heal from the mistakes your parents may have made with you. We always approached our children's biological families with compassion, trying to help our foster kids understand where they came from. The result was a greater understanding for the children and us as parents, as we recognized that people do their best with the available tools and skills. Even though you may not come from a background of trauma, you may have more compassion for yourself when you realize where you came from and how that impacts the decisions you have been making in your parenting.

Perhaps the most significant benefit to understanding your family history is that it can be passed down to your children. Take the time to explain to them where you came from and how things were handled in your family when you were a child. This can give your child insight into why you do the things you do for them and around them, lending them an increased sense of compassion for you and the generations that came before you. You can make this a fun family project that you work on together with some of the following tips:

- Interview family members about their upbringing.

- Complete a family tree project with a biography for each person.

- Allow your child to ask questions that matter to them.

- Keep it age-appropriate for your child. You may ask some questions privately until your child is old enough to handle sensitive topics.

As you make new choices that no longer reflect those of your family of origin, you pass down a new story to your child, which can be just as valuable. You can rewrite your core identity, connect with your culture, and ultimately reshape how you parent your child. You might have a few family recipes that have survived for generations, recipes that adorn the table of your holiday feasts and Sunday night dinners. Likewise, many people have family heirlooms that get passed from generation to generation as each child ages. However, that isn't the only thing you might pass down to your children. The path to poor parenting might be paved by the generations before you.

How did your parents punish you when you misbehaved or broke curfew as a child? Corporal punishment like spanking was common decades ago, but that isn't the only factor that could have had a lifelong impact on you. Even verbal reprimands, if delivered harshly, can verge into verbal abuse. Modern parents claim that they don't believe in these severe forms of punishment for their kids, but the survey results tell a different story. According to a 2013 Harris Poll, eighty-one percent of parents believed hitting their children occasionally was acceptable punishment. More than sixty percent claimed to have implemented this approach to parenting in their own home.

If we avoid discussing these types of corporal punishment, what compels us to act on them behind closed doors? We likely engage in these behaviors because we were raised with them. The University of Washington's Social Development Research Group pinpoints the dilemma. Parents raised under physical or emotional abuse will likely repeat the pattern when their children are born. These types of abuse can be traced through at least three generations, ensuring that the practices will continue in the present and future. Research at the University of Rochester Medical Center by Dr. Anne-Marie Conn found interesting results regarding adverse events in a parent's childhood. She and her team found that parents with multiple adverse events in their childhood, including beatings and spankings, were much more likely to choose corporal punishment for their children. This segues into other issues for the child, who is then subjected to a new generation of adverse events, including more emotional issues. For example, parents with four or more adverse childhood experiences were up to six times more likely to raise children with signs of emotional or social problems by the tender age of five.

So, how can you break this cycle? It starts with recognizing what you went through as a child and what your family considered culturally acceptable. Then, to make a significant change in parenting philosophy, seeking help to move past childhood wounds is essential. Family is more than a group of people. It is a complex network of relationships and interconnections. The family members are not just physically cohabiting in a house; they affect each other in deep and sometimes hidden ways formed by human emotions of love, joy, jealousy, guilt, happiness, etc. These interactions form the family attitudes and value system and constitute a big part of your childhood reality.

Toxic parents treat their children in ways that instill messages such as the following in them:

"You are not worthy."

"You won't amount to anything."

"You can't trust others."

"Your preferences don't matter."

"Don't express negative emotions."

"You can't live an independent life."

"You are not capable."

"Tough love is good, even if it hurts."

"Don't ask for help, it's dangerous."

"Arguing leads to trouble, better to give in and agree."

Families with toxic parents do not promote independence, self-esteem, or healthy boundaries. Instead, they create a toxic environment that teaches their members nothing but dependence on the parents, blurred personal identities, lack of trust, and emotional immaturity.

Repair or repeat!

When it comes to parenting, history indeed tends to repeat itself! For example, children of alcoholic parents are likelier to become alcoholics or marry alcoholics. Similarly, domestic violence victims are more likely to become future domestic abusers. But why is that? The primary reason is that we repeat our unrepaired (i.e., unresolved) experiences. At first glance, this does not make sense. Why should anyone repeat their parents' dysfunctional and hurtful behavior patterns?

Our childhood experiences affect us profoundly and sometimes unconsciously. The coping skills and behavior patterns we learn in our formative years become deeply entrenched. We tend to repeat them because they feel familiar, and we know how to deal with them. We might even think we can gain mastery over them if we try them again; it might be different this time! For example, the daughter of an alcoholic might marry another alcoholic, hoping she can save her husband and get the love and attention she didn't get from her dad. She might even think she deserves the neglect and misery because she was responsible for daddy's problems. For a child, it's easier to believe that she is guilty rather than that daddy (the protector and role model) is not trustworthy or flawless. We tend to repeat toxic parenting behaviors because they feel familiar and normal, and it's hard to change. As a result, we pass our childhood experiences down, even if we know they are unhealthy and hurtful. This cycle continues until we resolve the underlying trauma, change how we perceive and interpret our childhood experiences, learn new coping skills, and build new habits.

So, with everything we discussed in this chapter, is it possible to break the vicious cycle of intergenerational trauma? We can't change our genes. But we can certainly influence our epigenetics. We can't change the past. But we can indeed perceive our past experiences in fresh and different ways. You can repeat the cycle or resolve past issues and learn to break it. The first step to breaking the cycle is to remove the toxin. The next chapter explains this parenting detox!

Chapter Three

Parenting Detox

Children begin by loving their parents; as they grow older
they judge them; sometimes they forgive them.
Oscar Wilde, *The Picture of Dorian Gray*

Every parent is deficient in certain aspects. Sometimes these deficiencies become more severe, occur more often, and form behavior patterns or habits. As discussed in the previous chapters, our childhood experiences are vital to our parenting styles and habits. Parents with unresolved childhood experiences are vulnerable to reacting based on their inner pain when stressed. Their children do or say something, they get triggered and react to relieve their emotional discomfort, even if the reaction is not in their children's interest. Over time, this vicious cycle occurs and calcifies into toxic parenting habits.

The first step to stopping being a toxic parent is to identify such patterns and curb their growth and multiplication. Then, with the toxic habits cleansed, you can start forming healthier habits. This chapter focuses on unlearning toxic parenting behaviors, a sort of emotional cleanse, to begin with a fresh and revised perspective. You cannot set a clear path for new healthy habits without cleansing the old toxic ones. Self-reflection about your current behaviors, childhood experiences, and family history is the cornerstone of this emotional cleansing. That is because it's not our past that makes us, but how we perceive and interpret our past experiences. Take the example of Maya Angelou from the previous chapter. Her terrible childhood did not determine her adulthood fate. Instead, she transformed the pain of the past into fuel for future change. You might wonder how she could do that. Maya says in her poem, *On the Pulse of Morning*, "History, despite its wrenching pain, cannot be unlived. But if faced with courage, need not be lived again." Likewise, responsible parents dare to make a change for the better in their parenting. If you're reading about how to stop being a toxic parent, you have the will and the determination to be a responsible parent!

Toxic parenting is usually the outcome of a negative intergenerational cycle. To stop being a toxic parent, you should break this cycle. For me, breaking the intergenerational cycle means stopping being either a victim or the replicator of past traumas. You are a grown-up person now and have the freedom and power to change your life (at least in certain aspects and some levels). The most significant sources of childhood trauma are Adverse Child Experiences or ACE. The United States Center for Disease Control (CDC) defines ACE as any type of abuse (sexual, physical, emotional), experiencing or witnessing domestic violence, the sudden death of a parent due to murder, accident, or suicide, emotional or physical maltreatment, suffering from poor parenting by alcoholic or drug-addicted parents, and bullying, among others. Repetitive exposure to ACEs keeps the stress response system active for prolonged periods and disturbs healthy brain development, affecting future emotional regulation, stress response, and coping mechanisms.

CDC research published in 2018 shows that more than 60 percent of adult Americans experienced at least one ACE before turning 18, and a quarter experienced three or more ACEs. CDD researchers even believe this statistic is likely an underestimate of the vast magnitude of child maltreatment in the US. If you're alarmed by this data, the good news is that ACEs are preventable by breaking the intergenerational cycle, i.e., not passing our past trauma to the future generation and by adopting more supportive parenting and educational norms. Perhaps most of us have suffered some emotional damage at home or school, with family or friends. We can either keep carrying our baggage of unresolved emotional traumas or open the baggage, examine the stories inside, and free ourselves from them. Unfortunately, without self-reflection, we keep carrying the baggage and eventually pass it on to our children!

The self-reflection exercise

Your journey to stop being a toxic parent starts with self-reflections on your past and present. First, think about any ACE you might have suffered in your childhood. How was your life as a child? Were your parents nurturing, supportive, and patient? Did you enjoy going back home after school? Did you have a good bond with your parents? Do you remember instances of domestic violence or neglect?

Neglect is a hard-to-spot but common and primarily invisible source of trauma. Unfortunately, many parents don't realize they're traumatizing their children when they don't support or comfort them in times of distress. Here is an everyday scenario: The child makes a mistake, especially in public; they bump into something or drop something, or are too slow, etc. Instead of comforting them first, the parent blames the child, making them feel even worse. Toxic parents repeat such scenarios time and again, exposing their children to multiple mini-ACEs. Neglect leads children to believe that they are unworthy of love and attention. They internalize the pain, humiliation, and loneliness, thinking it's their fault.

Toxic parents are usually authoritarian. They shame and humiliate their children into submission and expect them to accept the treatment. They don't care about their children's needs and show little empathy for them. In her 1980 book *For Your Own Good: Hidden Cruelty in Child-Rearing and the Roots of Violence*, the world-renowned Swiss-Polish psychologist and philosopher Dr. Alice Miller says, "We don't yet know, above all, what the world might be like if children were to grow up without being subjected to humiliation, if parents would respect them and take them seriously as persons." If you are an adult who experienced neglect and humiliation in childhood, please know that you can start to process your trauma, find your self-worth, and model a different parenting style with your children.

Unfortunately, many parents get too self-critical during their self-reflection journey. Bringing some painful memories back to life can make us feel helpless and frustrated, wondering what's wrong with us. But you can reflect without judgment when you realize you were not responsible for what happened. So, please be kind and patient with yourself.

The other part of your self-reflection process is to examine what infuriates you as a parent. Then, you might be able to link past experiences and present behaviors easily. Otherwise, some help from a trauma-informed therapist will be very beneficial. Toxic parenting patterns start with single events when parents get irritated, upset, outraged, or helpless. Once repeated over and over, those reactions form patterns and habits. Triggers are the events or situations that drive the parents mad or helpless. In other words, you get triggered when your child does or says something making you excessively angry or annoyed. Whining, tantrums, back-talking, non-compliance, and crying are among the most common triggers. We'll talk about triggers later in this chapter.

I recommend getting help from licensed therapists or counselors in your self-reflection journey. They can help you recognize your past traumas and current triggers, normalize the trauma, and make you feel heard, understood, and supported. Don't go it alone! A good therapist can identify unhealthy habits, accelerate healing, and teach healthy coping using proper therapy techniques. In my self-reflection journey, I used Narrative Exposure Therapy (NET) to go through my childhood chronologically and review the pleasant and unpleasant experiences. This gave me to have a more thoughtful reflection by reconstructing positive memories alongside the traumatic ones. There are multiple other therapy techniques to heal emotional trauma. A licensed therapist is more qualified than me to advise you on this topic.

Parenting detox 101

So far, in this chapter, we talked about self-reflection to help you know yourself better. Armed with that knowledge, you can proceed with your parenting detox. Let's begin with the basics; the most common toxic parenting behaviors you should avoid; in other words, the low-hanging fruits of better parenting. At this stage, forget about being a great parent or role model or establishing an incredible bond with your child. It is essential first to stop making obvious parenting mistakes. If you manage to do that, you're already ahead because you have stopped the toxin at its source. Over time, you can remove the already-generated parenting toxin and then go to the next stage to develop healthy habits and a solid parental bond.

Here are some of the most common toxic practices familiar to many parents:

- Putting your interests before your child's

- Yelling

- Shaming your child

- Excessive control

- Blaming

- Withdrawing affection or attention through ignoring or the silent treatment

- Disciplining out of anger

- Being too judgmental or comparing your child to others

If you engage in one or more of these behaviors, you need to make some changes! Whether it is caused by burnout or a laundry list of things gone wrong, lousy parenting habits tend to stick much more effortlessly than good ones. Maybe it's because they are easier than controlling your anger or emotions.

By this point in the book, you have probably recognized some toxic behaviors and traits in yourself. So, what to do now? Fortunately, there are many actions you can take to start unweaving the tangled web of toxicity. In my experience, there are three general categories of actions for parenting detox:

Initiation: These steps will initiate the process and put you on the right path to stop being a toxic parent. The goal is to know the situations that trigger your toxic behaviors, reflect on them, and link them to how you react to your child.

Implementation: These steps focus on facing daily struggles, being prepared, keeping the momentum, adapting, and dealing with setbacks without giving up.

Endurance: The final set of steps is to keep moving steadily, compound the learnings to keep the toxicity away, and build alternative, healthy, and positive parenting practices.

In the following section, we'll review the essential steps in each category. But before that, let's do a visualization exercise! For your parenting detox journey, imagine what kind of parent you didn't like to have when you were a child. Nobody likes a stressed-out, impatient, yelling, blaming, killjoy, unreliable, or disengaged parent. So, try not to be one! Remember, parenting starts with you, not your child. If you're at peace and capable of regulating your emotions, you have a shot at being a good parent.

So, first, focus on yourself. Here are some guidelines to help you do that!

Revisit and revise your parenting beliefs and expectations

Many parents get triggered because their children's words, actions, or behaviors don't meet their expectations. In other words, their children do not comply with their parental rules (their "do's" and the "don'ts"). Our parental rules come from our parental beliefs. For example, if you believe your children should accept your views because you know more or better, any disagreement can trigger you. Similarly, you won't tolerate their desire for independence if you think children should be seen but not heard. A collection of self-centered, manipulative, or abusive parental beliefs (such as those discussed in Chapter 1) provide fertile soil for toxic parenting behaviors. So, if you would like to stop being a toxic parent, you must do some self-reflection, revisit your parental beliefs and revise them if needed.

The first step in this self-reflection process is to examine your family beliefs, rules, and dynamics. As mentioned in Chapter 2, how you were raised plays a crucial role in how you raise your children. Think about your childhood and search for dysfunctional family characteristics, such as too much control, perfectionism, abuse, blame, and rejection of negative emotions. For example, think of a highly-educated father not accepting anything other than becoming a doctor or lawyer or no grade lower than A. If your parents expected you to obey them no matter what, keep them happy, make them proud, etc., chances are high you'll expect the same from your children. How we were raised and treated by our parents forms the basis of our parental value system. Without revisiting and revisions, we'll repeat the same behaviors and impose the same rules on our children because of our inherited beliefs.

Let's review a few more examples. When parents are pissed off and withdraw affection, their kids learn that they have to keep their parents happy to be loved by them. Hence, the following belief gets ingrained in them: "You're loveable if you obey your parents." The kids grow up and have children of their own. You and I are past children turned into parents! If you still believe children should not argue or disagree with their parents, you've set yourself up for drama and disappointment. On the other hand, if you believe disagreement is a normal part of any relationship and even needed to develop independent identities, you will embrace it with a peaceful mind.

Another typical parenting misconception is that discipline equals punishment. This is a misconception because discipline is about educating and instructing good behaviors. Here is what Merriam Webster Dictionary says about the origin of discipline: "Discipline comes from discipulus, the Latin word for pupil, which also provided the source of the word disciple. Given that several meanings of discipline deal with study, governing one's behavior, and instruction, one might assume that the word's first meaning in English had to do with education." Punishment and blame are the most accessible tools to damage the relationship with your child. Toxic parents think of discipline as punishing their children when misbehaving, not teaching them or modeling good behavior. For example, imagine you spank your child because of their behavior. Wouldn't they wonder why it's OK for you to hit them but not for them to hit their siblings or friends? Wouldn't that teach them that aggression is OK to reach their goals? In a healthy family, parents set clear and reasonable limits and communicate them to their children. They explain the underlying reasons and are flexible enough to adapt and compromise. They try to influence, inspire, and encourage their children, not control them. So, if you think you can discipline your children even if it hurts them, think again! Put yourself in their shoes. Are you encouraged to behave well after being punished, blamed, belittled, or hurt?

Another example is how parents react to their children's feelings. Do you believe children should control or hide their emotions, especially negative ones such as anger, sadness, or frustration? In *For Your Own Good: Hidden Cruelty in Child-Rearing and the Roots of Violence*, Dr. Alice Miller says, "The greatest cruelty that can be inflicted on children is to refuse to let them express their anger and suffering except at the risk of losing their parents' love and affection." If you don't like to be a toxic parent, try to provide a safe environment where they can express their emotions without feeling insecure.

When children cannot recognize and communicate their emotions, they express them physically by throwing tantrums, frowning, screaming, stomping, fist-clenching, throwing objects, hurting themselves and others, etc. Likewise, when parents are not emotionally intelligent, they are prone to parenting stress and unhealthy coping mechanisms. Emotionally intelligent parents consider their child's negative emotions and misbehaviors as teachable moments for themselves and their children. On the other hand, emotionally immature parents take offense and issue punishment! Which approach do you prefer?! Revisiting and revising your parenting beliefs will change your mindset, help you bridge the gap between reality and expectations, and decrease parenting stress. So, take some time and reflect on your parenting behaviors.

Know your triggers and reflect on them.

We briefly talked about triggers earlier in this chapter. Any parenting situation that makes you feel outraged, upset, helpless, very sad, or out of control is one of your triggers. I suggest considering what triggers you and choosing the most common or hurtful ones for the next detox steps. Knowing your triggers helps you think through the situation when it inevitably arises again and allows you the space to plan how you would like to respond in similar situations. Imagine your child is nagging. You might react in different ways. For example, you can give a funny answer, distract your child, and playfully stop the nagging. Alternatively, you can get pissed off, start shouting, blame your child, and ask them to stop. Your child did the same in both scenarios, but your reaction was very different. Getting triggered by an event or situation is more about how you perceive or interpret it. In other words, getting triggered is more about you and how you process the emotions caused by your child's behavior. Excessive anger or frustration is to alleviate our emotional discomfort. Hence, to understand why we get triggered, we should find out why a particular situation is emotionally painful for us.

But why do we get triggered? What is the source of our triggers? According to Dr. Daniel Siegel, professor of psychiatry at the UCLA School of Medicine and the renounced author of multiple parenting books, our triggers originate from unresolved childhood experiences. Professor Siegel says the following in his 2013 book Parenting from the Inside Out: "Issues rooted in our past impact our present reality and directly affect how we experience and interact with our children even when we're unaware of their origins."

Facing emotionally unpleasant situations, children develop coping strategies, i.e., ways to protect themselves and survive the family or school environment. For instance, imagine a boy whose parents or other caretakers did not allow him to express negative emotions, mocked him for crying, or expected him to be always happy because (in their eyes) he had everything. This boy learned to hide his negative emotions as a defense mechanism. However, when he grows up and becomes a father, he can get triggered by his child crying or whining if he doesn't resolve the frustration or anger he experienced in his childhood. Similarly, if our imaginary father was neglected when he was bored or upset in his youth, he can feel helpless and sad when his child starts whining or throwing a tantrum. This is how the intergenerational cycles and epigenetic mechanisms discussed in Chapter 2 function.

Knowing your triggers is a fundamental step in stopping parenting toxicity. Some parents recognize their triggers easily. Others might need professional help and counseling sessions. After identifying the triggers, you need to do some homework to resolve the underlying factors. For example, when I went through my counseling sessions many years ago, I realized any criticism or complaint from my son was one of my triggers. I took it as a personal attack because I believed I was doing my best to provide a good life for him. Then I remembered how my dad treated me in precisely the same way. He was a hardworking teacher who used to do side hustles for extra income. We were not allowed to complain about anything at home. Otherwise, he would be outraged and start shouting and lecturing us about how hard he worked and how lucky we were! It took my counselor several sessions to help me realize that I am no longer a child and have the power and freedom to behave differently with my son. It took me a while to change how I perceived the complaints from my son. I gradually managed to let him speak up without getting pissed. When I responded less and listened more, I realized that he was complaining about all sorts of subjects but not about me! After a while, I considered those "complaints" as part of everyday communication and was not triggered by them anymore.

Knowing your triggers allows you to respond consciously, not react unconsciously. In addition, it makes you much more supportive and empathic because it diminishes your emotional discomfort and separates it from your child. A parent who is not triggered can stay in control and respond like an adult. Once you know your triggers and start resolving their underlying reasons, you can control your impulses. In addition, you will gain the awareness that you're being triggered. So, although you might still get upset or angry, you will not take it out on your child.

Keep learning and take it slowly and steadily.

Unlearning toxic parenting requires effort and consistency. Expecting yourself to make significant and lasting changes at once is unreasonable. It will take time, even if you are dedicated to this new lifestyle and motivated to control your impulses. Remember why you're trying to improve your parenting when it gets challenging. When children suffer years of toxic parenting, they lose so much trust in their parents that any attempts at healing the relationship might fail miserably. I've witnessed some of my foster kids unwilling to amend their relationship with their biological parents. You might face the same challenge with your child, especially with teenagers, and if the toxic parenting was ongoing for years. So, please be patient and take it slowly but steadily. If you face significant resistance from your child, choose an activity of their interest and try to have some fun together.

Good communication is essential in this journey, for example, sharing your feelings or informing your child that you are working on becoming a better parent who yells less or gives in less frequently to the same behaviors that have characterized your relationship with them. When your child knows you are working on becoming a better parent, it also gives them the space to improve.

Don't forget to take care of yourself. You are taking a giant step toward better parenting, which takes a lot from you. How can you break longstanding behavior patterns, learn new skills, control your impulses and triggers, and offer gentle care and attention if you're not in good shape (physically, mentally, and emotionally)? Just like the airplane oxygen mask (put them on first before helping others!), you should first take care of your well-being before you can properly parent your child.

I know (out of experience) that you'll have several "Aha!" moments in your parenting detox journey.

When you notice your triggers and examine your parenting beliefs and family history, you will understand your thoughts, behaviors, and shortcomings play the most significant role in your parental issues. At that stage, you'll realize the need to change, heal past traumas, revise some of your beliefs, and learn new skills.

Much of this process is self-work. But you might need the assistance of a trauma-informed therapist to resolve some of the past issues. Maybe you prefer attending parenting conferences and reading books to support your journey toward healthier parenting. However, others might do better with one-on-one coaching with a trusted therapist or counselor. I've found both methods helpful and have witnessed countless other parents engage in therapy with excellent results. It might even be a good time to enlist the help of a family counselor who can work with you, your partner, and your child to develop a new family dynamic.

Connect more, correct less!

There is a vast difference between correcting your child and criticizing them. This is perhaps one of the best things you can learn to break the cycle of toxic parenting. All parents should issue corrections for their children to help them learn healthy boundaries. However, resorting to harsh criticisms to motivate them would be counter-productive. Never call your child names or criticize who they are as a person. Instead, help them problem-solve and devise a reasonable solution for the situation. For example, bad grades might necessitate hiring a tutor or attending extra classes. It might even be a sign of a deeper issue, for example, problems with classmates, bullying at school, or family problems at home. Think of yourself as your child's lawyer, a professional, compassionate lawyer with good intentions! A good lawyer will guide and advise their client, explains different options and their consequences, and supports and protects their clients whenever needed. Of course, the parent-child relationship is much deeper, and none of the parties is replaceable! Nevertheless, a similar dynamic applies, with some extensions.

The goal is for parents to guide their children to a more successful and acceptable outcome. Therefore, while you may still need to issue discipline, it should be done with problem-solving in mind. While all parents must sometimes issue corrections and reprimands, many toxic parents struggle with excessive reprimands. It can be tempting to reprimand your child in the heat of the moment, but this often leads to ineffective punishments that are overly harsh for the situation. I know I have been guilty of doing this with my kids. It's tempting to see a situation and then issue a punishment immediately so that you can begin to move past it. However, you may see more clearly with some time away. The first step to controlling reprimands is to calm yourself before disciplining. This lets you get clear and consistent on what the punishment entails and how to enforce it.

When you do need to reprimand your kid, keep it short and sweet. Giving a few clear and concise statements is better than giving a long lecture. Your child is more likely to retain and understand why their behavior was unacceptable if they don't have to sift through a ton of words and judgments about it. I have a rule of thumb for my parenting lectures! I call it the One-to-Ten rule, which means for every word I say, my child should get the opportunity to respond and explain ten times as much. It's basically me trying to talk less and let them open up and talk more. I highly recommend trying this rule of thumb, and I'm sure you'll be surprised about the outcome. Last summer, we were on a short trip with some of our foster kids. We went for a short stroll in the local market. One of our kids (an 8-year-old) immediately started nagging and complaining about how tired he was. It was getting annoying for everyone since we had just started walking, and there was no way he could tire so fast. It was tempting to start blaming and trying to shut him up, especially because this was not his first time ruining our day out by nagging. Instead, I asked him why he was so tired. After some hesitation, he opened up and explained he felt pain in his right heel. When I took him for a medical examination a few days later, the doctor told us that he had a mild form of Sever's disease, which causes swelling and irritation of the heel. My 8-year-old son did not know about his heel problem; he thought he was tired! It took several minutes of gentle talking to find out he was not acting up or nagging. I felt relieved and happy that I managed those moments like a good lawyer, not a toxic, stressed-out, impatient parent!

Do I always manage to be a good "lawyer" for my kids? Not at all! Every child is unique, and every situation is different. Sometimes I've failed miserably and had a terrible feeling of incompetence and regret afterward. But, after many years of trial and error, I've realized that instead of looking for blueprints and exact recipes for parenting success, we better keep some general principles in mind to handle difficult parenting situations. These principles should be simple enough to remember in challenging moments and detailed enough to be actionable. They act like a compass to show the general direction; the exact route will depend on the unique hurdles along the way. So, let me explain some of my general principles to connect before correcting my kids.

Always explain why your child is being punished with a calm and respectful tone, being as firm as you need to be. Avoid yelling, name-calling, and other actions that could border on verbal or emotional abuse. Belittling your child is not likely to have the desired effect on their behavior and can increase shame, further perpetuating the intergenerational cycles of toxicity in your child. Instead, it is better to find positive things to say about your child, showing them what to do instead of focusing on what not to do. We will talk more about this in Chapter 6 when we discuss positive parenting.

If you are stuck in a cycle of constant reprimands, it might be time to spend a little one-on-one time with your kid. For example, one of our more challenging children and I had a problematic relationship. I constantly reprimanded him for everything: not cleaning up, poor grades, a lack of initiative in school and at home, and a messy room. The only way I could break the cycle we found ourselves in was to find an activity we could spend time together doing that would benefit both of us. Sometimes, we would go out for ice cream. Other times, we might play a board game or make dinner together. The key was to avoid negativity and focus on my son's positive attributes. When I found ways to be intentional with time spent together and praising him for things he was doing well (there is always something your child does well), we broke the cycle of constant reprimands. I used positive reinforcement to strengthen his good behaviors and gradually replace the less desirable ones.

One of the most effective ways to stop the toxic parenting cycle is to replace punishment with negative reinforcement. Negative reinforcement is the reinforcement of the desired behavior by removing an aversive stimulus. For example, the constant beeping sound you hear when you sit in your car and don't wear a seat belt is an excellent – and annoying instance of negative reinforcement. In contrast, punishment is to weaken a particular behavior. For example, a teacher can eliminate the homework if students work hard in class and get good grades (negative reinforcement by removing an undesirable stimulus, i.e., the homework). But, on the other hand, the teacher can also give more homework if the students get poor grades (positive punishment by adding an undesirable stimulus, i.e., more homework). So, remember that reinforcement is to strengthen good behavior and is fundamentally different than punishment.

Unfortunately, many parents mix up negative reinforcement with punishment. While they intend to reinforce a behavior negatively, they end up punishing their child and miss the reinforcement aspect altogether. Punishment is similar to reinforcement; since it could include adding or removing a stimulus. The key here is to understand that reinforcement, whether positive or negative, is to strengthen a behavior. Constant punishment is one of the most common parenting pitfalls and a significant contributor to lousy parent-child relationships. By learning various reinforcement techniques, you can decrease or even eliminate punishment and make your parenting life easier, happier, and healthier.

Another way to minimize reprimands is to stop situations before they devolve into a scenario where you must criticize your child. If you see a situation going sideways, get creative and issue a distraction. This is particularly helpful with younger children, but teens can benefit just as much. For example, change the topic quickly, play a game with them, change the setting by going for a walk with them, or ask them to complete an activity with you. No matter what you find most helpful for your child at their given age and developmental stage, a distraction can be highly beneficial to re-establish a positive connection with them and minimize the impact of a less-than-desirable situation.

Don't get toxic again!

At times, it will become evident that you are stuck in a parenting rut and unable to do anything to correct it. Patterns like toxic parenting can be deeply ingrained. They tend to reappear even if you have managed to bring them under control for a while. If you find yourself falling into a pattern of toxicity, such as too much yelling, overly strict or harsh discipline, withdrawing love and affection, or shaming, you aren't alone. Parents can start to get out of a rut by listening to their children and asking them to share their thoughts and feelings. This is an opportunity to validate the child's feelings and forge a genuine connection with them. Find ways to allow them to express themselves and supply them with coping skills for big emotions. By reinforcing healthy habits for the child, parents can simultaneously begin to internalize those same skills when they feel overwhelmed or out of control. It can be a fun way for parents and children to connect when both struggle to free themselves from a deep rut of intense emotions or withdrawal.

Even if you don't feel like it, another way to get out of a parenting rut is to display love and affection toward your kid. You may not feel like loving a child who misbehaves or pushes all of your buttons. But it can help reset the relationship. Instead of yelling or disciplining, pull them in for a big hug. Offer to play a board game or help them with homework. Spending quality time or being affectionate with your child will reset your connection and help you be gentler in your parenting.

Another way to break free of a parenting rut, particularly one involving excessive anger, is to redirect your child. For example, instead of yelling when they do something wrong, simply correct them with a note that what they did was unkind, rude, or impolite. Then, give them an example of a time when they were the opposite of those things (kind, respectful, or polite). This gives them a chance to reflect on things they do well, allows you to acknowledge something good about them, and sets the stage for both of you to move forward in a more positive headspace.

Parenting detox requires much effort, patience, knowledge, reflection, and consistency. So, don't expect to have overnight success. Most parents need several detox cycles since the life circumstances, their children, and themselves change constantly. Parenting is hard, and you can't resign from it! So, why not learn to do it better? Parenting toxicity is hurtful and damaging to the parents too. It prevents them from growing and enjoying their parenting journey. So, think not only of your child but also yourself if you get tired and decide to stop trying.

Getting yourself out of toxic parenting habits requires diligent and consistent work. It starts with something straightforward, though it can be challenging when you are in an emotional headspace: Be emotionally present for your children and pay attention to their thoughts and feelings. So often, they act in a way that triggers your anger or other emotions because they need someone to take the time to hear their concerns. So hold the space for them and allow them to share what they need to express, providing alternatives to help them cope more positively with their feelings.

You should see noticeable improvements in your parent-child relationship once you have the basics of parenting detox. When you reach that milestone, it's wise to reinforce the newly-established dynamic, reflect on your achievements and experiences, and think about the next steps. The following chapter will help you regulate your emotions better, visualize your desired parenting life, and the relationship you love to have with your child. You could become a better parent and more desirable person at the end of this process! Sound fantastic? Let's find out how to get there!

Chapter Four

Emotional Regulation for Better Parenting

If there is anything that we wish to change in the child, we should first examine it and see whether it is not something that could better be changed in ourselves.

Carl Gustav Jung

Most parents wonder why their kids give them such a hard time. So they focus on managing their children's behavior and making them more compliant. But unfortunately, in most cases, the parents' outcome is failure, frustration, power struggle, and missing out on enjoying the early years of having children. Let me ask you a question: Based on what we've discussed so far, knowing that parenting starts with you and children mirror their parents' reactions, don't you think we should focus on managing our reactions and behaviors instead of theirs?

In the previous chapter, we talked about parental beliefs, rules, and triggers. Those are all related to you and have nothing to do with your child. Instead, your personality traits, past experiences, and perception of the world around you form how you think, feel, and behave. So, how about shifting the focus from managing your child to managing yourself?! I've witnessed surprisingly calm and connected parents who never get pissed off, yell, or go out of balance while interacting with their children. Of course, you might say those are lucky parents with easygoing and cool-tempered kids. But how about parents with disabled, sensitive, and easily-frustrated children or single parents on low incomes? How do they manage to stay in control despite their difficult circumstances? I'm sure you've encountered such parents and might have even envied their peaceful attitude! So, what is their secret? What can we learn from them? In my experience, their secret is managing themselves well; in other words, how they perceive and react to their children.

This chapter concerns one of the most crucial parenting skills: managing yourself! The goal is to be mindful of your parenting reactions, especially when you're tired, stressed out, or in a hurry. Managing yourself doesn't mean stopping to experience negative emotions. Instead, the focus is on how you react to those emotions. For example, when mindful, you can still get angry at your child. But you won't act out of anger. Unfortunately, toxic parents control or manipulate their kids rather than manage themselves. In your journey to becoming a desirable and loving parent, you must learn to regulate yourself and practice mindful parenting. Hopefully, this chapter will be your guide and companion in this journey!

Mindful parent, mindful child

Numerous scientific studies have shown that negative interactions with your child increase their distress. No surprises, we already knew that! If you're like me, you might have been prone to emotional reactions up to and including anger when things didn't go according to plan. The more intensely I reacted to something, the more likely my son responded to me with equally intense and harsh emotions. It took me a long time to unlearn the pattern I inherited from my parents and extended family. There is much to learn here; your child can benefit from your emotional management. So how does emotional management teach your child through osmosis?

Perhaps most importantly, your kids can learn that you don't have to respond to every situation equally with chaos and out-of-control behaviors. Even toddlers can recognize when parents are calm, collected, and in control. Not only does this make them feel significantly safer with you, but it also teaches them a better way to manage their distress when it arises. Your kids are seeing up close and personal how to handle difficult emotions, and they can apply those lessons to their own experiences with anger, frustration, despair, etc. Learning from an early age how to handle big feelings is a valuable skill that can be best taught via behavioral modeling. Even if you try to teach your child through reading books or lecturing, it won't be nearly as effective as how you respond to your emotions.

Don't take this to mean that you should hide all of your emotions from your child. The idea here isn't to mask all of your feelings but to take control of them. Children are intuitive and can sense when someone isn't genuine. Simply putting on a happy face because that is what you believe your child wants or needs don't teach them the value of managing their emotions. The trick is letting them see your emotions but not overwhelming them with out-of-control behaviors surrounding those big feelings. For example, allowing your child to know they messed up and you're disappointed is okay. However, scolding them, calling them names, or verbally abusing them to handle anger isn't okay.

Realize that your children aren't giving you a hard time. They are having a hard time navigating their emotional experiences, and they look up to you for a role model, whether you want to be or not! When you have yours under control, you teach them a valuable lesson on how to manage theirs. Even if you have to take a break to handle your anger, it can be beneficial for your child to see that you can calm yourself to deal effectively with a situation. This can encourage more openness and honesty in the relationship with your child. It shows that you can handle your emotions and can serve as a safe space for them to experience their feelings with you by their side.

Faking emotions, being authentic, or none!

A central question to emotional regulation is how to express emotions to our children. For example, should we hide, disguise, or show negative emotions such as anger or frustration? Or should we exaggerate our positive emotions? In most cultures, parents are advised to hide their negative emotions from their children, keep their composure around them, and pretend to be strong and in control. Many parents think that emotional regulation equals masking their feeling from their kids, but this is a misunderstanding. Hiding your feelings from your child does not teach them what it means to regulate their emotions and might even ingrain their belief that feeling sad, angry, worried, etc., is unacceptable.

Even if we do our best not to let our children see what is happening behind the scenes in our brains, they can still pick up on the nonverbal cues we inadvertently put into the world. It causes them to respond on a visceral level that can dramatically impact them. They may even feel that they cause your disengagement, signaling the need to change how they act around you, even if your negative emotions or anger have nothing to do with them. It's OK to let your kid know you are upset, but frequently losing your temper can produce severe consequences for your child. They might feel like they are the root cause of your frustration, leading to stress and physical changes in their brain development. Researchers from the University of Montreal found that children raised with harsh parenting techniques developed a smaller prefrontal cortex and amygdala than children who didn't. Both structures play a significant role in emotional regulation and the development of anxiety and depression. So even without physical abuse, not managing your emotions properly has a detrimental impact on your child.

Numerous studies show that suppressing negative emotions damages parents' well-being and the parent-child relationship. Furthermore, hiding negative emotions is mentally taxing; it takes the energy parents could spend to attune to their children's needs. Hence, when parents try to withhold or disguise their negative emotions, they often appear disengaged, distracted, non-responsive, and even rejecting. The truth is that we don't do a good job of hiding our feelings anyway. Even if we think we are managing it on the surface, other telltale signs arise and cause our kids to become just as stressed as we are. So emotional suppression backfires almost every time.

How about positive amplification? Should we amplify our positive feelings to support, praise, or reassure our children? A 2016 study by researchers from the Department of Psychology at the University of Toronto in Canada shows that positive amplification is mentally taxing in the same way as suppressing negative emotions and has some of the same effects, such as lower responsiveness and diminished relationship quality. So the bottom line is that faking our feelings for our kids isn't the way to go; it's mentally taxing and doesn't teach emotional management to children. Early in my fostering career, I always tried to behave like company CEOs around my kids; I was always energized, in control, and had a solution for every situation! But soon, I realized I couldn't continue that way because it was emotionally and mentally draining, and my kids kept coming to me even for the most uncomplicated issues. Hence over time, I tried to be more emotionally authentic. But then I discovered I shouldn't show my genuine anger or frustration because that's even more damaging! Anger is the most common trigger for parents. They find themselves yelling, mostly when they're angry. The critical point to understand here is that anger doesn't appear independently. Instead, it originates from underlying emotions such as fear. Imagine your child ignoring their homework. You might get angry because you're afraid they'll fail at school and ruin their life. I don't think it's a good idea to be honest here and tell them what you genuinely believe and feel.

So, if it's not advisable to fake emotions around our children or show them what we genuinely feel, what should parents do?! Dulling our emotions or dumping them unfiltered on our kids are both undesirable. The alternative is regulating our emotions and expressing them after processing and filtering. For example, imagine you're very sad. Then, it is OK to sit down and cry in front of your young children only if you take the following steps:

- Explaining how you feel,

- Mentioning sadness is a normal feeling, and it's OK sometimes to feel sad,

- Clarifying that it's not their fault,

- Explaining that you'll be OK,

- Pulling yourself together soon,

- Comforting them if needed.

In this scenario, you showed your authentic feeling in a controlled, moderated, and educational way. You were true to yourself while keeping your child's interest in mind. You taught them it's OK to feel sad and how to handle it. But, of course, if you're weeping every day, you better seek professional help and not involve your children!

But how about more challenging feelings, such as anger? What if your child pisses you off? How can you regulate anger, show it constructively, and create a teachable moment? Let's consider another scenario. You've brought your five-year-old son to a playdate at his best friend's house. You've been there for several hours; now it's time to go home. Your son doesn't like that, starts screaming and kicking, and calls you a mean mommy. How ungrateful could a child be? Right? Perhaps you feel furious and unappreciated after spending all that time on him! Isn't it tempting to shout at him, force him to get going, and show who the boss is? But hold on a minute! The meaning you assign to your child's behavior (which originates from your parenting beliefs and rules) plays a significant role in how you feel in such situations. If you believe he is ungrateful, you expect him to behave like a grown-up, which he's not!

On the contrary, if you consider that he's really sad because he has to stop playing with his best buddy, you'll have an entirely different take on the situation and become much more empathic toward your child. As mentioned earlier in this chapter, realize that your son doesn't give you a hard time, he's having a hard time! Your fury will distress him even more without teaching him how to cope with his grief other than kicking and crying. At age 5, your son is very much driven by his emotions and needs your help to learn how to deal with frustration. If you tell him something like, "You're having a good time, and I know it's hard for you to stop, but we need to go. We'll have another playdate soon." What if he keeps shouting and kicking? Children often use whatever strategy they can to get what they want, and they watch your reaction! A mindful parent won't reinforce the defiant behavior by giving in or getting angry. Instead, they show empathy, acknowledge and understand their child, ignore provocative behaviors, and control their reactions. This is an effortful exercise but gives constructive feedback to the child and models good coping and communication skills.

The simple truth is that parenting is hard, and keeping cool while tired or upset is difficult. Not everyone is lucky enough to have family around to help with the kids or have good-tempered and easygoing children. I see my parenting life as constant course correction and emotional balancing. I am not a perfect parent; I get triggered occasionally. But I try to regain my emotional balance and reconnect with my kids quickly. I think it's OK to open up to your children and show your emotional struggles and vulnerability, but in a controlled and educational way. I am sharing this to say you're not the only parent dealing with doubts, failures, daily struggles, and setbacks. Just keep learning and moving forward, do your best, and take it not too hard on yourself!

Emotional regulation 101 for parents

Nobody is born with the ability to regulate their emotions. Instead, we learn it throughout our lifetime and can constantly strengthen it. Regulating emotions is primarily about being aware of our emotions, how they affect our behaviors, and how to handle them. Emotional management is essential to give you the peace and space you need to have improved interactions with your little one. You can take some simple steps to deal with your feelings more appropriately while modeling for your child what healthy emotional management looks like. You may find that when you can get yourself under control, you stand a better chance of your kid having control of their emotions.

The following tips and tricks will help you change your emotional response and build up resistance when responding from an emotional headspace. You might be surprised that many of these tips have nothing to do with your children and their behavior. That's because if you're healthy and have a balanced life, you'll better manage parenting challenges. The general premise of this book is to first focus on yourself, make sense of your past experiences, try to heal your emotional traumas, and have a healthy and fulfilling life. Otherwise, we'll just pass our crap to our kids! But, of course, the same applies to emotional management. So first, learn to manage your emotions. Then, maybe you'll succeed at becoming a good emotional mentor for your kids.

It can take a Herculean effort to keep calm amid your child's emotions and behaviors, but it is necessary to succeed at stopping toxic parenting. Self-regulation allows you to look at a situation objectively, understand that it isn't always about you, and respond from a calm place. The rest of this chapter presents five tips to help you regulate your emotions. This is by no means an exhaustive list. But they are the essential ones, based on my experiences. Always see what works for you and what doesn't, and choose your way ahead.

Take care of yourself

Self-care (emotionally, physically, and mentally) is essential to emotional regulation. Think of all the basic stuff anyone (parent or not) should do to improve their quality of living. Here are some examples:

- Treating physical illnesses,

- Getting exercise

- Sufficient and high-quality sleep

- Having a balanced diet

- No smoking or excessive drinking

- Engaging in healthy activities that bring you joy, etc.

Parents, especially those with young children, are usually so busy that they forget to care for themselves. Parenting starts with you, so ensure you are healthy and happy to care for your family. Otherwise, you will become angry, resentful, stressed, and unable to give good care. Realize that taking care of yourself is not selfishness. For example, if you spend time on a good message and pedicure instead of being with your child all the time, you are not being selfish. On the contrary, you do yourself and your family a huge favor. Even taking small chunks of time daily to reset and relieve stress will significantly help. Think of what works for you; yoga, meditation, watching movies, reading a book, listening to music, etc. Do not forget physical activities. Even simple activities such as walking or cycling can enormously help. Regardless of what you do, try to spend some time every day, so you can handle parenting challenges gracefully instead of feeling trapped and worn out.

Recognize the underlying feelings

As mentioned before, anger is the most common trigger for parents. They find themselves yelling, mostly when they're angry. However, anger does not always exist in a vacuum. Often, secondary emotions such as shame, jealousy, helplessness, embarrassment, or frustration accompany anger and are even more powerful. If you can cope with these other emotions, you may stand a better chance of handling your anger efficiently. Anger is a protective emotion; in other words, it's how our brain reacts to protect us from the emotional discomfort caused by the underlying emotions. For example, imagine you're downtown walking with your daughter. Suddenly she lets go of your hand, runs toward a toy store, trips over, and almost smashes into the shop window. Instead of comforting her, you instinctively get angry when you reach her again. That's because you feel helpless and worried that she might have hurt herself. Anger is the expression of how you feel beneath the surface. You can think of anger as an emotional iceberg; most of the iceberg is hidden beneath the surface!

Physiological symptoms do accompany anger. By being present in your body, you can notice warning signs that anger might be getting ready to erupt. You can do this by quickly checking your body and how you feel. For example, notice if you experience a faster heartbeat, tense shoulders or jaw, clenched fists, and more intense sweating. If you feel the early signs of agitation, it's time to do what you can to minimize your anger now before it explodes. Once outside the situation that sparked your fury, it is vital to self-reflect and figure out what went wrong. What was it that set your anger off? Did your child talk back to you, ignore you, or become blatantly disrespectful of your parental authority? Understanding what sets you off is vital to minimizing outbursts and angry reactions. Once you know what buttons your child will push to trigger your anger, you can better manage similar situations in the future.

Pause before reacting

Often, anger prompts us to react to our kids instead of responding with care and intention. It tells us that we need to speak or act right now, leading us further down the path of toxic parenting. Instead of simply reacting to your child, take a beat to think through what you will say or do next. The best thing to do here is to pause before you respond to them in any way. You can tell your child you need a minute and then leave the room to get your physiological symptoms under control. Whenever possible, take a longer break to allow yourself to respond with empathy and understanding; read a chapter from a favorite book, take a hot shower, go for a walk, etc.

Handing out discipline in the heat of the moment can be tempting, but this is often not the best solution. Wait until you know what an appropriate reaction would be if your child deserves one. We had one challenging foster child who sparked my anger with his backtalk and constant disrespect. I doled out punishment in the heat of my anger, and he ended up grounded for almost two weeks over nothing more than a simple homework assignment! I had to go to him later, apologize for my reaction, and recant the punishment to something more appropriate for the problem. This is an example of why it is not in your best interest to issue discipline in the heat of the moment. It is also a good time to commit to never using physical force like spanking, especially when angry. You should never turn to corporal punishment, no matter how much your child eggs you on.

Not sure that you can respond in a pleasant way to your child? Put yourself in time-out for a little while. If you struggle to maintain your positive mood and upbeat demeanor, you should give yourself a few minutes away. Young children might need you to stay close by so that you continue supervising them. But with older children, you can step outside momentarily, head to the bathroom or even just lay in bed for a few minutes. Consider asking another family member or partner to watch over your child if you need to take a time-out.

This is one area that took me a lot of practice on my journey to more mindful parenting. I was always tempted to deal with the situation at the moment and as soon as possible. I learned to pause, even for a few seconds, to think about what I wanted to say and why before it crossed my lips. A brief pause helped me respond more rationally and logically without fueling the fire of my child's dysregulation. When you are tempted to respond quickly to get the situation over with faster, take a ten-second pause, a deep breath, and then respond more mindfully.

Accumulate positive emotions

Add some positive self-talk into your repertoire of skills. Tell yourself that you aren't going to react mindlessly to your child. Give yourself some praise for noticing your anger and reducing your emotional reaction. This is also a great time to try some visualization techniques that put you in a better frame of mind. Picture yourself responding calmly and patiently instead of in chaos and anger. Visualizing is a powerful tool to help you act in a stressful situation. Imagine yourself in a relaxed mood. Even if your child triggers you, you probably won't lash out. What if you could stay in a relaxed mood more often?

Engaging in joyous activities is another way to recharge your emotional battery. These could be activities you do well and enjoy or something you enjoy with your child. One way to boost yourself from your negative headspace is to do something completely unexpected. For example, when we were having a rough week with one of our children, we threw a party on a Wednesday night just to break through the tension. We ate Hot Pockets for dinner, blew up balloons, and wore fake mustaches. The silly break from a chaotic environment filled with anger and hostility was just what everyone in the family needed to move past a difficult season.

Whatever nourishes you, spend more time engaging in that activity, and it will help you regulate overwhelming emotions when they pop up while parenting your child. For example, I know that I am a much better parent when I take the time to exercise and rest. When I'm tired or have too much pent-up energy, I am more likely to respond from a place of frustration instead of unconditional love, confidence, and acceptance.

Despite our best efforts, we often fall short of parenting expectations for our children. For example, you will sometimes lose your temper with your child over a hot-button issue. What do you do when this happens? You can take the high road and admit to your child that what you did and how you responded was wrong. Issue them a genuine apology to demonstrate your remorse.

This takes the first steps to start repairing your relationship with your kid and sets a great example of what it means to make a mistake and ask for forgiveness.

Get more proactive and less reactive!

Most parents are reactive; they act in response to the situation. The problem with being reactive is having no time to process our feelings, analyze our assumptions, and act rationally. The outcome is reacting hastily and instinctively. Proactive parents are more prepared and try to change or create more desirable and predictable situations. For example, the morning hour when everyone is getting ready to go to work or school is usually hectic and stressful for many families. You can take some steps in preparation for that hour, such as getting clothing and school items ready, waking up a bit earlier, and accommodating your routine to your children's quirks. You can do the same for other daily situations, such as going out to the playground, playdates, dinner time, bedtime, etc. You can use the same recipe to prepare for every situation: you know your child and their quirks, predict what can go wrong based on past experiences, and think of strategies to make the situation less stressful or more pleasant.

You've heard this sentiment before: choose your battles wisely. The truth is that not everything your child does or says against you is worth your anger. Sometimes, you can ignore the situation and know it will take care of itself. Choosing your battle is another form of being proactive;

you decide when and how to react. For example, one of my foster kids would routinely smear peanut butter on the counters while making his lunch for school in the mornings. Cleaning up his messes every morning, before I had even had my first cup of coffee, infuriated me and set us up for failure from the very earliest moment of the day. We had a rocky relationship, and this simple thing wasn't worth the battle day after day. Could he clean up the peanut butter? Yes, he was certainly capable. However, it wasn't worth putting our relationship in jeopardy every morning. As a result, I learned to save my discipline and firm hand for more important issues.

As your child gets into their teenage years, they will start having opinions different from yours. Let your child know their view is valuable and that you care about their opinion. Even if it differs from yours, listen quietly and calmly while they tell you about it. The truth is trying to argue or force your opinion usually does not help. Instead, simply be present and hold space for them to be themselves. Every child needs emotional presence from their parents. They don't need us to be available non-stop but in some connecting moments. This could be as simple as ignoring other distractions, making eye contact with your child, and focusing on what they have to share with you. When you proactively provide attention, empathy, and affection, they don't need to act out or push you to get them from you.

Proactive parents create a space between the stimuli and responses, giving them the headspace to consciously process and regulate their feelings, control their impulses, and respond rather than react. Conversely, reactive parents limit their options and are pushed to act mindlessly based on their raw emotions. Proactive parents focus on preparing for less stressful interactions, and reactive parents constantly try to repair a struggling relationship and wonder why they never get it right! Which one do you like to be?!

Chapter Five

Know Your Parenting Personality

All of our experiences fuse into our personality. Everything that ever happened to us is an ingredient.
Malcolm X, The Autobiography of Malcom X

One of the most common reasons for toxic parenting behaviors is acting based on our unfiltered personality traits instead of what is best for our children. For example, suppose your personality is decisive, willful, and authoritative. In that case, you may have a more strict approach to parenting and fall victim to toxic parenting behaviors, such as being overly critical and rigid. On the other hand, you might be a very nurturing parent who is susceptible to being overly controlling and trying to "fix" your children with extreme care. Many parenting behaviors are highly dependent on personality traits, for example, the default attitude towards discipline and time management, the degree to which they involve themselves in activities with their children, communication styles, how they handle criticism, openness to change, etc. There are several personality types, each of which has unique strengths and weaknesses when dealing with children. Therefore, knowing your type can help you identify which areas you may need to develop to become a better parent. Understanding your parenting personality helps you become more mindful and intentional in your approach. For instance, parents aware of their tendency towards rigidity and inflexibility could start working on more flexible rules and boundaries. On the other hand, if your parenting personality is more permissive, you may need to create more structure and enforce boundaries more consistently.

One of the easiest and most reliable ways to know more about your personality traits is to take a personality test. Personality tests consider psychological preferences to determine how individuals interact with others, make decisions, and handle emotions. These tests can help parents uncover the traits that make them unique, such as whether they are introverted or extroverted, risk-takers, or more laid-back. Knowing these traits can help parents recognize their tendencies in parenting. For example, a parent may be too hard on their children or lenient. Knowing these tendencies can help them make conscious, informed decisions and help identify areas that need improvement.

In the previous chapter, we discussed knowing your triggers and creating a space between the stimuli and responses to regulate your emotions. If you know your natural tendencies, you are better equipped to recognize what triggers you and how to respond mindfully instead of reacting instinctively. This chapter focuses on various personality types and traits and how they affect parenting approaches. The goal is to help you reflect on your traits and identify and curb detrimental or ineffective parenting practices. We'll review the most widely used personality tests and how to interpret them in the parenting context. At the end of this exercise, you will know yourself better and have a clearer idea of where to focus your efforts to become a better parent. Personality tests are valuable tools for self-discovery. However, they should not be taken as perfect indicators of toxic parenting because toxic behavior can happen in any personality type. What personality tests can do is highlight specific tendencies which make us prone to certain toxic behaviors.

Personality tests for parents

If you like to take an objective look at your parenting style, I suggest you take one or more of the following personality tests: *Five-Factor Model* (also known as the *OCEAN* model), *Myers-Briggs Type Indicator (MBTI)*, and *Enneagram*. Let's first review each of them in more detail.

The Five-Factor model, aka the "Big Five" or OCEAN is a widely used and scientifically-proven model of personality traits. It is based on several individuals' pioneering works, including D.W. Fiske (1949) and L.R. Goldberg (1993). This system uses five broad dimensions to characterize various personality traits: Openness to experience, Conscientiousness, Extraversion, Agreeableness, and Neuroticism. This model touches on the essential aspects of who you are and can be immensely helpful in determining what areas you need to work on to achieve a more pleasant parenting experience. It is designed to help you easily uncover core personality pieces and provides accurate feedback on improving your interactions with the people around you, including your child. The Big Five test is freely available on various online sources.

The Myers-Briggs Type Indicator (MBTI) is a widely used and well-known personality assessment tool developed by Isabel Myers and her mother, Katherine Briggs, in the mid-20th century based on the theories of psychologist Carl Jung. The MBTI is based on the idea that each person has a unique personality type, made up of a combination of preferences in four dichotomies: Extraversion (E) vs. Introversion (I), Sensing (S) vs. Intuition (I), Thinking (T) vs. Feeling (F), and Judging (J) vs. Perceiving (P). The MBTI assessment involves answering a series of questions that measure these preferences and provides an individual with a four-letter code, such as ESTJ (Extroversion, Sensing, Thinking, and Judging), to represent their personality type.

Each MBTI type is an acronym representing four of the eight possible preferences that an individual might have. The first preference is either Introversion or Extraversion, which is the extent to which an individual is energized by interacting with others. The second preference is either Intuition or Sensing, which is the function individuals primarily use to take in information. The third preference is thinking or Feeling, which is how individuals make decisions. Finally, the fourth preference is either Perception or Judgment, which is how individuals structure their lives.

The Myers-Briggs approach focuses on external, observable behaviors, an individual's attitude toward life, how we perceive and process information, and how we interact with our environment. For example, people with the ESTJ personality type tend to be outgoing, action-oriented, practical, systematic, and organized. In addition, they are logical and goal-oriented and often make decisions based on facts and data rather than emotions. You can take the MBTI personality test online on the Myers-Briggs Company website (MBTIonline.com) or use various free online versions (e.g., www.16person alities.com).

The Enneagram system consists of nine personality types and is based on the teachings of the South American philosopher Oscar Ichazo in the mid-20th century. Ichazo believed these are nine distinct world views and strategies people use to relate to themselves and the people around them and cope with their environment. The Enneagram assigns a nine-point type based on the individual's responses to questions about internal experiences, such as motivations, values, and fears. The premise is that each person has a unique set of core motivations and needs. Here are the nine Enneagram types and their main characteristics.

Type 1: The Reformer (principled, purposeful, self-controlled, and perfectionistic)

Type 2: The Helper (generous, demonstrative, people-pleasing, and possessive)

Type 3: The Achiever (adaptive, excelling, driven, and image-conscious)

Type 4: The Individualist (expressive, dramatic, self-absorbed, and temperamental

Type 5: The Investigator (perceptive, innovative, secretive, and isolated)

Type 6: The Loyalist (engaging, responsible, anxious, and suspicious)

Type 7: The Enthusiast (spontaneous, versatile, acquisitive, and scattered)

Type 8: The Challenger (confrontational, decisive, willful, and domineering)

Type 9: The Peacemaker (receptive, reassuring, complacent, and resigned)

We can bundle these personalities (based on their commonalities) into three categories or triads: the "instinctive" triad (Types 1, 8, and 9), which reacts to their gut instincts, the "feeling" triad (Types 2, 3, and 4) which cares about their emotions and self-image, and the "thinking" triad (Types 5, 6, and 7) which tends to think and even worry. There are various online Enneagram tests, both paid (e.g., the Riso-Hudson Enneagram Type Indicator) and free. The paid tests usually are more comprehensive and provide more detailed test results.

Overall, the Five-Factor Model (OCEAN), MBTI, and Enneagram can all be valuable tools for understanding your personality and finding a parenting style that works for you. In addition, these tests provide unique insights into your psychological makeup and the motivations behind your parenting decisions. Therefore, I highly recommend taking at least one of these tests and using the feedback to become a better parent (and a better version of yourself!). Our focus here is not on these tests. Instead, we want to use the insights gained from the tests to improve your parenting style.

Once you've completed one or more personality tests and have the results, you can use the feedback to understand your default parenting preferences. In other words, you can deduct your parenting personality, i.e ., how you interact with your children, based on your personality traits. When it comes to parenting, different personalities lead to different parenting preferences. For example, people with a Myers-Briggs ESFJ (Extroverted,

Sensing, Feeling, Judging) personality type are usually caring parents focused on providing their children with a secure and structured environment. On the other hand, ESTJ (Extroverted, Sensing, Thinking, Judging) personalities are more authoritative and may emphasize the importance of rules and discipline. People with the INFP (Introverted, Intuitive, Feeling, Perceiving) personality type make gentle and understanding parents willing to listen to their children and provide emotional support and guidance. Meanwhile, an ISTJ (Introverted, Sensing, Thinking, Judging) parent is usually a highly organized and reliable figure who cares about hard work and practical skills.

Toxic parenting can occur in all personality types. However, some personal traits and tendencies lend themselves better to toxicity. Realize that these tendencies are not written in stone. We can change and balance our qualities with self-awareness and effort. Additionally, it's important to remember that toxic parenting behaviors can result from various factors such as childhood experiences, cultural background, and parenting beliefs, not just personality type. However, having certain personality traits make it more effortless to get toxic. How to interpret the outcome of each personality test in the parenting context? We'll cover that in the next section.

Big Five parenting profiles

This system uses five broad dimensions to characterize various personality traits: Openness to experience, Conscientiousness, Extraversion, Agreeableness, and Neuroticism. Each dimension is measured on a continuum scale between the two extreme sides of the spectrum. Let's check each dimension in more detail.

Openness to Experience

When given the opportunity, do you jump at the chance to try something new, or do you hang back and wait to see what the results are for others? Parents who score high in this category tend to be open to new teachings (hopefully like the ones in this book!) and more likely to explore their feelings. If you are thinking about embracing more mindful and connected parenting, this is a great trait to have. You may find implementing some of these changes easier because you are more open to them. On the other hand, parents who score low on openness to experience tend to be hesitant to make changes and are generally more conservative. Low scores on openness to experience may indicate a tendency toward rigidity and inflexibility, leading to a lack of creativity and rigid adherence to strict rules and expectations for children. An openness to negative feedback and criticism can be lacking in toxic parents, who may be unwilling to consider alternative points of view or critical information.

Conscientiousness

Do you tend to think about every action before you make a final decision? Or are you a bit more cautious when making a change? Perfectionists often score high in conscientiousness, with a high degree of self-discipline. If you score high in this category, you are more likely to set goals for yourself and meet your objectives. Conversely, scoring low on conscientiousness signifies impulsiveness and reacting based on anger or frustration. As a result, toxic parents may be more likely to be careless with their parenting responsibilities or fail to provide consistent, firm boundaries.

Extroversion or Introversion

Most people don't need much of an explanation in this category. Parents who are social and crave interaction with others rate high on extroversion. It's important to note that parents who score high in this category love interacting with others, including their children. They want more pleasant social interactions, which makes them more dedicated to putting these parenting practices into their skills rotation. Because of your outgoing nature, you might assert dominance in interactions, even with your child. Some extroverted parents crave attention and validation, which can lead to neglecting the needs of their children in favor of their social desires and needs. An overly extroverted parent may be intrusive, excessively dominating, and not give their child the space and privacy they need. If you prefer to spend time by yourself, and this is how you recharge, then you would rank high on introversion which is the flip side of the coin. Sometimes, you might find that there is a shadow side to introversion. Introverts may not be all that interested in what is happening in the lives of those around them. You may not be interested in spending that much time with others, including friends, family, and your child.

Agreeableness

Agreeableness relates to how likely you are to agree with others instead of giving your opinion or making choices. If you score high in this category, you may get caught up in what others want from you. As a result, you are likely to embrace changes that come your way, even if they are not your first choice. Agreeable people are often described as friendly, kind, and pleasant. As a parent, this has another side, though. You might get caught up in the storm of your child's emotions and get carried away with them. This makes setting boundaries with your child more challenging because you want to be agreeable to whatever they want. Low agreeableness can lead to irritability, lack of empathy, and harsh behaviors. Such parents can come off as a bit cold or unfriendly. This may give them the space needed to set necessary boundaries with their child, but it can also make them less likely to adjust to their child's requirements. It may be more of a challenge for them to respond lovingly, even if they do love their child immensely. A lack of agreeableness may lead to parents who are overly strict, unkind, or unwilling to listen to their children.

Neuroticism

This is one area where you may want to embrace a low score, as neuroticism tends to refer to your propensity to experience negative emotions. It often manifests as insecurity, anxiety, over-protectiveness, or even parental inadequacy. Conversely, parents with high levels of neuroticism may be prone to damage a child's self-esteem by their moodiness, irritability, or overreacting. Scoring low on neuroticism makes you more likely to approach novel situations calmly and securely. You may not be as bothered by the little things that pop up occasionally, and you are likely to respond to them with logic instead of emotion. Feelings don't tend to run as high if you score low in this category. Because you are less emotional about what happens, you tend to be secure in who you are and your parenting.

MBTI parenting profiles

As mentioned before, each MBTI type uses an acronym representing four of the eight possible preferences that an individual might have: Extraversion (E) vs. Introversion (I), Sensing (S) vs. Intuition (I), Thinking (T) vs. Feeling

(F), and Judging (J) vs. Perceiving (P). Regardless of their personality type, all parents might demonstrate some toxic traits if they are not self-aware and don't strive to be caring and considerate of their children. Each MBTI type has positive and negative traits, and awareness of both is essential. For example, knowing about the negative traits helps you recognize your potential triggers and proactively develop the space between what your child does or says and how you respond. Let's review the most common toxic parenting traits for each MBTI type.

ESTJ parents are often demanding and inflexible, expecting their children to conform to their rules and decisions. They may also be overly controlling, micromanaging their children's lives and not allowing them to make their own decisions. They can be inconsistent, changing rules and expectations without warning, critical, and never satisfied with their children's accomplishments.

Some traits associated with INTJs, such as a strong need for control and a tendency to focus on logic over emotions, can sometimes lead to toxic parenting behaviors, such as overly critical and rigid. Therefore, INTJs must balance their natural tendencies with a supportive and nurturing parenting approach.

INTPs prioritize intellectual pursuits over emotional connection. Furthermore, their tendency to be detached and impersonal can sometimes lead to toxic parenting behaviors such as emotional neglect and a lack of warmth or affection. Instead, INTPs should try to understand their children's emotional needs and provide a warm, caring, and emotionally attuned environment for them.

ISTJs value order and stability and may be overly strict in enforcing parenting rules. This could result in a lack of flexibility and an unwillingness to consider alternative approaches. Similarly, they are resistant to change and may be unwilling to consider new approaches to adapt to the changing needs of their children as they grow and develop.

ESFJs may be overly protective of their children, hindering their development of independence and self-reliance. They value conformity and may expect their children to follow the rules and fit in with others. This could result in a lack of support for their children's interests and desires. In addition, ESFJs may discourage their children from expressing negative emotions or may dismiss their feelings altogether, resulting in an unhealthy emotional climate within the family.

ISFJs are often nurturing and caring but may have trouble setting boundaries and enforcing discipline. This could result in permissive parenting and a lack of structure for their children. In addition, they might lack the flexibility to accept new views and adapt to changes. Hence, they might struggle to meet their children's evolving needs and interests.

ESTPs are known for being impulsive and living in the moment. They sometimes make poor decisions without considering the long-term consequences of their actions as a parent. They might consider themselves honest and direct. But they might end up crossing boundaries and hurting other people's feelings. ESTPs may struggle with setting boundaries and providing structure for their children, which could result in a lack of discipline, neglectful behaviors, and a chaotic home environment.

ISTPs are often seen as detached and may have difficulty expressing emotions or showing affection to their children. This could result in a lack of emotional connection with their children. In addition, they tend to be practical and focus on short-term needs resulting in hasty or thoughtless decisions regarding their children's future.

ESFPs are often seen as spontaneous and may make decisions without considering the consequences. This could result in inconsistent or irrational parenting decisions. For example, they may prioritize having fun over creating a stable and structured environment for their children, which could lead to a lack of boundaries and discipline. ESFPs are also prone to self-centeredness and neglecting their children's needs and feelings.

ISFPs value emotional connections and may have trouble separating their emotions from their children's experiences, which could result in over-involved or intrusive parenting. Furthermore, they may struggle to establish consistent rules and routines, leading to confusion and a lack of structure for their children.

ENTJs are natural leaders and can be highly competitive. They may tend to be overly controlling and assert their authority in their parenting, resulting in a lack of independence for their children. They are results-oriented and may have trouble understanding the emotional needs of their children and showing empathy. ENTJs can have high expectations and may push their children to perform at a high level, which could result in unnecessary stress and pressure.

INTJs prefer reason over emotion and might overlook the emotional impact of their actions on their children. This could result in a lack of warmth and compassion in their parenting style. In addition, they often have high expectations for themselves and others and may apply this same standard to their children without accommodating their needs and strengths.

ENTPs may over-stimulate their children by simultaneously exposing them to too many new experiences and ideas. This could result in a lack of stability and structure essential for a child's development. In addition, they are often more focused on logical thinking and may be perceived as unempathetic and struggling to understand their children's emotions.

ENFJs tend to express emotions intensely, which could be overwhelming for their children and lead to feelings of guilt or shame. They are often warm, caring, and nurturing individuals, but they may be overly involved in their children's lives. This could result in a lack of independence and an inability to develop critical thinking skills.

INFJs are empathetic and skilled at understanding others' emotions, which can lead them to use this ability to manipulate their children's emotions. This could result in a lack of trust and difficulty developing children's

emotional intelligence. They might also project their beliefs and desires onto their children instead of accepting
their individuality.

ENFPs are often enthusiastic and nurturing peo-
ple-pleasers and might avoid confrontation and disciplining their children, even when necessary. Similarly,
they might struggle with setting and enforcing boundaries with their children leading to a lack of structure and
accountability and harming the child's development and
self-sufficiency.

INFPs may experience strong emotions and may have
trouble regulating their emotions. This could result in
mood swings and inconsistent parenting, which is con-
fusing and unsettling for their children. On the one hand,
they are often nurturing and compassionate, which can
lead to overprotectiveness. On the other hand, INFPs
may avoid confrontation when feeling emotionally ex-
hausted, making it challenging to address problematic
behaviors or set clear expectations.

Enneagram parenting profiles

The three instinctive types—the Reformer, the Challenger, and the Peacemaker—all strive to create an environment of safety and contentment for their children.
Reformers, in particular, are known for their ability to
set clear boundaries and instill discipline. Challengers are
known for their frankness and directness and often set
clear expectations for their children. Finally, peacemak-

ers are compassionate and understanding and prioritize harmony and peace at home.

Type 1, the Reformer, focuses on 'good' and 'right' behavior, which leads them to be overly strict, controlling, and demanding. This can manifest in punishment, criticism, over-involvement, and micromanagement to ensure everything is perfect. Type 8, the Challenger, may have a 'my way or the highway' approach to parenting, emphasizing control and authority. They can be overly aggressive and authoritarian, leading to a hostile and oppressive atmosphere. Type 9, the Peacemaker, can be too passive and gentle, often neglecting to set boundaries and rules. They may also be too accommodating, leading to a lack of structure.

The three feeling types (the Helper, the Achiever, and the Individualist) all strive to build strong, loving relationships with their children. Helpers are very nurturing and caring and often rely heavily on their instincts to make decisions. Achievers often have high expectations and focus on providing their children with the best possible opportunities. Finally, individualists are known for their independent thought and encouraging their children to think critically about the world around them.

Type 2, the Helper, may also be overly controlling as they often feel the need to 'fix' their children and try to mold them into a particular image. They may become excessively invested or enmeshed in their children's lives and emotions, often smothering them with extreme care or manipulating them through guilt and affection.

Type 3, the Achiever, often prioritizes success and accomplishments over everything else. This can lead to an environment that pressures children to succeed, strive for excellence, and always be 'the best.' The Achiever parents usually lack empathy and are prone to prioritizing image and success over their children's well-being and happiness. Type 4, the Individualist, may be inclined to emotional outbursts and criticism, leading to a tense and unpredictable atmosphere. They are typically susceptible to criticism and can take it personally, leading to overreactions and lashing out at their children.

The three thinking types (the Investigator, the Loyalist, and the Enthusiast) all focus on giving their children the analytical and critical thinking skills necessary for success. Investigators are highly analytical and strive to equip their children with the knowledge and skills to succeed. Loyalists focus on teaching their children the importance of loyalty and responsibility and often emphasize the need to question authority. Finally, Enthusiasts are creative and often give their children much freedom.

Type 5, the Investigator, can be too detached from their children, focusing more on intellectual pursuits than emotional ones. They may also become overly controlling and rigid to ensure that their children meet their high standards for order and accuracy. Type 6, the Loyalist, can be anxious and prone to over-protectiveness and fear of the unknown. They may become overly controlling and try to shield their children from potential dangers. Type 7, the Enthusiast, may become too lenient and permissive, neglecting to set clear boundaries and rules. They may also try to do too much and be over-involved in their children's lives.

After learning about these personality types and their shortcomings, you might feel depressed that you cannot make a good parent! As Mark Twain said in his 1889 essay, The Memorable Assassination, "No man has a wholly undiseased mind; in one way or another, all men are mad." So we're all deficient in one way or another, and parenting is a great way to bring these deficiencies to the surface. Perfect parenting is impossible. But despite our shortcomings, being a wise and caring parent is indeed possible.

While personality tests such as the Big Five, MBTI, and the Enneagram can provide valuable insights into one's tendencies and preferences, you should not see them as the determinants of your parenting fate. We're dynamic and ever-changing entities and can adopt new mindsets and attitudes. The personality tests show our intuitive and automatic mechanisms to interact with the world around us, including our children. Each personality type has specific positive attributes to make wise and caring parents and some weaknesses. The goal here is to recognize our weak spots and approach parenting with empathy, flexibility, self-reflection, and willingness to grow while prioritizing the well-being of our children.

Have you experienced periods of seemingly great parenting being interrupted out of nowhere? The routines that have worked great so far stop working, siblings react entirely differently to your parenting, failing to keep up with the ever-changing needs of your children, etc. Parenting is like a game with constantly changing rules. That's why staying attuned to your child is so critical. That's the topic of our final chapter!

Chapter Six

Staying Attuned to Your Child

I believe that what we become depends on what our fathers
teach us at odd moments, when they aren't trying to teach
us. We are formed by little scraps of wisdom.
Umberto Eco, Foucault's Pendulum

So far, we've explored the making and behaviors of toxic parents, unlearning the most common toxic parenting practices, emotional regulation, and the relationship between personality traits and parenting preferences. You have enough knowledge to stop being a toxic parent by this point. That's a critical milestone, but it is not enough!

Parenting advice might sound logical and doable until you're deep in the parenting trenches, fighting the daily battles over all the big and small hassles your children throw at you! One of the questions I have had for a long time in my parenting journey was why so many good-intentioned parents fail. Imagine you've managed to get rid of the toxicity in your parenting. Does that mean your success is guaranteed? Not at all! You might still struggle with defiant behaviors and challenging temperaments. It is as if parenting is trying to shoot an agile, ever-moving target!

It took me many years to learn parenting starts with us, but it's not all about us! It's a two-way street between you and your child, a bidirectional relationship. Most parenting advice (including much of this book) circles around what you, the parent, should do, which is all fair and helpful. But it's not the whole picture. Think of parenting as a game of ping-pong between you and your child. How you hit the ball affects their reactions and vice versa. In other words, you can think of parenting as an endeavor you take with your child or a journey with your child as a fellow passenger. In many daily situations, your child acts in a particular way, and you react, which causes them to show yet another reaction. This game of parent-child ping-pong goes on every day in countless homes worldwide.

Children affect their parents even before birth, forcing them to make many adjustments for their arrival. Babies dominate their parents' lives, for example, their sleep quantity and quality, stress level, mood, and propensity to psychological conditions such as anxiety and depression. A growing body of scientific data shows that children sometimes influence their parents even more strongly than parents influence them. This phenomenon is called "bidirectional parenting." An essential outcome of bidirectional parenting studies is that parents of children with challenging behaviors resort to more strict and authoritarian parenting. The opposite is also true; children who show good behaviors receive warmer and calmer parenting reactions. Many studies show that defiant and oppositional children push their parents to adopt harsher parenting practices. I am sure you have similar experiences when a nagging and oppositional child has driven you crazy and forced you to take strict measures you usually avoid. This might be a relief after all; it might ease some parenting pressure and guilt!

If you have more than one child, you might be surprised by how different they could be. Children raised by the same parents and in the same environment could be vastly different. That's because every child is unique and interacts uniquely with their parents. We should not forget that every child has a different genetic makeup, specific temperament, sleeping pattern, social and emotional characteristics, and needs. A 2015 meta-analysis of fifty years of twin studies examining more than 14 million pairs of twins revealed that identical twins raised apart were more similar than fraternal twins raised in the same home. The main takeaway of this enormous study was that the genetic disposition of a child plays a significant role in their behaviors. Does this mean that nature beats nurture? The jury is out on this topic. However, most psychological experts believe both are important and focus on their interaction, for example, via epigenetic mechanisms.

So, do all these mean that parenting doesn't matter that much?! That's definitely a misinterpretation! Parenting matters immensely, but it doesn't happen in isolation. The child's characteristics could evoke different parenting behaviors, impacting the child, causing specific parenting reactions, and this circle continues! That's why parenting is so hard, and many of us feel we never get it right!

This last chapter of the book puts all the previous learning into the context of the parent-child bidirectional relationship. The goal is to internalize the key concepts and help optimize and adapt them to your situation. The central theme of the chapter is parenting while staying attuned to your child. You are the adult, the role model, and ultimately accountable for responding maturely to your child. If you stay attuned, the parenting journey will become less stressful and, hopefully, more enjoyable.

So, how can you parent your child with love and discipline without being too harsh and toxic? We'll review seven general guidelines to help you stay attuned to your child, act as their advocate, be more mindful, and never get toxic again. The common thread in these guidelines is to parent in such a way that you make fewer mistakes and, even more importantly, recover faster and easier from the parenting mistakes you'll inevitably make. In the end, perfect parents don't exist, but wise and caring parents do, and you can be one of them. Let's find out how!

Model healthy behaviors and attitudes.

Once you become a parent, many of your daily experiences become mutual. Your child observes your actions and reactions and reflects them on you like a mirror. For example, if you use demeaning language around your children, prepare yourself to be embarrassed by your child repeating them afterward, probably at the wrong times. The good news is that this goes both ways. If you exhibit good behaviors and display healthy habits, your children will learn more than they ever will from your words. Children have an eye for your emotional shifts and try to mimic them, and since they cannot express their feelings well, they look to you for ways to express themselves. Hence, if you're expressing your frustration by lashing out or choosing to yell and become distant when faced with difficulties, chances are so will your kid. This mimicry keeps the intergenerational cycles going, both the toxic and the positive ones.

Breaking the toxic cycle and creating a new and positive one requires conscious and intentional effort. Perhaps the easiest way to start a healthy and positive relationship with your child is to take care of yourself. Once you become a parent, caring for yourself and your needs becomes challenging, especially when your child is very young. However, your children will follow if you prioritize your health and do what makes you happy. Your little one, seeing you do something for yourself, such as reading, exercising, eating healthily, or learning a new skill or hobby, will try to mimic and emulate you. You can't expect your child to handle their big emotions if you fail to regulate yours. Similarly, if you never talk about your feelings and show that it's OK to feel sad, frustrated, or angry, how can you expect your kids to know your emotions and learn to handle them calmly?

The character of the parent-child relationship changes as the child grows. In their early years, children are copycats and mimic. In their pre-teen years, they start to behave independently but are still heavily under your influence. So, you should remain mindful of your words and actions. One of the mistakes I've seen with many parents is that they try to influence the everyday choices of their children, such as their clothes and hobbies. This is more common with pre-teens and teenagers. Modeling healthy behaviors is more about instilling fundamental values and healthy habits. Friends and peers have a more significant influence on daily choices and actions.

Take the following daily scenarios and think about the questions:

A father spends his evenings watching TV or on social media. Can he expect his son or daughter to use their free time wisely, read more, or learn to play a musical instrument?

- Mom and dad argue every day over all sorts of stuff. Can they expect their children to get along well with one another?

- A mom lectures her kids to be respectful but shouts at sales assistants if they don't accept a return or argues with the dentist receptionist when she is late for her appointment. Do you think her children will believe in her lectures?

- A father becomes entirely detached or furious to cope with stress and frustration. Can he expect his son to fare better in stressful school situations?

The bottom line is that parents should demonstrate the behaviors they would like to see in their children. It is naïve and unrealistic to think we can change our children. But because of the mutual parent-child interaction, we can influence them by regulating what we do and say. Parents who intentionally try to model good behaviors might get surprised by the profound changes in their behavior. When your behavior reflects how you want to set an example for them, you become gradually and steadily more patient under challenging situations, more understanding of others, more thoughtful of your actions, and mindful of your interactions with people. Children can also remind us to stay aware of our environment and community and demonstrate the importance of values like respect and kindness. Generally, our behavior becomes more conscious and intentional because we hope to set a good example. So, while we try to change how our children behave, we will probably become a better version of ourselves.

Practice empathy and try to understand your child's perspective.

Oxford Dictionary defines empathy as "the ability to understand and share the feelings of another," for example, your children. Think of empathy as putting oneself in their shoes, trying to understand why they might feel a certain way, and then expressing understanding and support for their feelings. Empathy helps children feel secure, accepted, and understood and is essential to build trust and to develop a healthy parent-child relationship. Practicing empathy towards children is not an easy task. It requires patience, compassion, and attention to your child's emotions. Empathic parents look for cues in their children's behavior, body language, and words that may indicate feelings such as frustration or exhaustion. They also give their children time to process their feelings and explain their perspectives.

So, how can you become a more empathic parent? First, when your child is upset or angry, don't try to offer advice immediately or rush to a solution before hearing them out. If you manage to do that, there are multiple other ways to be more empathic. Here are some examples:

- Active listening: Pay attention to the child's words and try to understand their feelings and perspectives. We'll discuss active listening in more detail later in this chapter.

- Showing interest in their feelings: Ask questions and validate their emotions.

- Putting yourself in their shoes: Imagine how they feel and respond accordingly.

- Encouraging them to express their feelings: Create a safe and supportive environment to share their thoughts and emotions.

- Practicing empathy in your life: Lead by example and show your children how to empathize with others.

- Showing understanding and compassion: Offer comfort and support when they are upset, and acknowledge their experiences.

- Refraining from judgment: Avoid criticizing or

blaming them and try to understand their actions and feelings.

If your child struggles with low self-esteem, you can try to boost their self-esteem and self-confidence by catching them in the act of being good. As parents, we too often only acknowledge our children when they are doing something wrong. If you want empathy for their weaknesses, one technique is to shore up their strengths, acknowledging your child when they do well, even if it is just something small. Find multiple things to praise daily and watch your child's self-esteem soar.

Caring parents want to get deep beneath the surface to see the unanswered needs. You acknowledge the pain and discomfort of your child in the hard-to-love moments with empathy, caring, and compassion. Instead of reprimanding them immediately, you meet them with tender love, fostering a sense of resilience. According to research from Harvard University, "relationships with caring adults can turn toxic stress into tolerable stress." You can meet your child with what they need at any moment, recognize their pain, and take steps to heal it.

Finally, it is essential to be open-minded. Children will have different outlooks and perspectives, and it is necessary to respect these. By trying to understand their views, parents can show their children that their feelings are valid and that they are heard. This can help build trust and foster an atmosphere of openness and understanding between parents and children.

Show love and affection regularly.

We had a foster son who demonstrated some challenging behaviors: kicking holes in the wall, breaking electronics, screaming at the top of his lungs, and being disrespectful, to name a few. At first, we met each of these challenges with reprimands and corrections until we realized there was a better way to connect with him. We adhere to the idea that kids who are most difficult to love are the ones that need it the most. As a result, we changed our methods and met challenging behavior with love. We would give hugs, show affection for him, and offer an alternative. Most often, that alternative was a snack or one-on-one activity. He had come from a background where food was scarce, and hunger triggered him to act out in ways that weren't acceptable. He needed to know he was loved, safe, and cared for in our home. The difference that this approach made in his challenging behaviors was remarkable. He became cooperative, cheerful, and helpful with consistent, caring love.

Caringly loving your child alters their perception of the world and is crucial for their emotional growth and even the physical development of their brain. In addition, it allows them to heal from past toxic parenting. Researchers from Washington University in St. Louis have done some fascinating work on how the brain develops. They discovered that love from mothers spurred brain growth at twice the rate of growth seen in neglected kids.

They saw faster growth in the hippocampus, the part of the brain most associated with learning, memory, and stress response. While children should get this caring love as early in life as possible, there are still benefits to adopting it as soon as you learn about it.

As I shared in my story of one of my foster sons with some challenging behaviors, caring love dramatically changed him. He began to thrive when he felt accepted and understood, and we started meeting deeper needs. In addition, knowing he was loved and accepted improved his self-confidence and made him less concerned about what the future might hold for him, decreasing his stress levels.

Is it enough to instinctively love our children? The world is changing fast, families are becoming increasingly nuclear, and work-life balance is getting more challenging. All these factors make instinctive parenting, i. e., simply following our gut feelings and hoping for the best, less effective. Instead, I believe parenting love in the modern age should be more intentional, caring, and purposeful. Intentional love for parenting is unconditional, adaptive, aware, and compassionate love for our children. It involves emotional support, understanding, and patience, setting appropriate boundaries and expectations, affirming children's growth and development, helping them build self-confidence, and encouraging independence. It also teaches children positive values and life skills while creating a safe and secure environment. Intentional love inspires a trusting relationship with your children and creates a sense of security that helps children make healthy choices, cope with stress, and build strong relationships.

Getting rid of toxic parenting traits does not happen automatically. Instead, it requires a lot of soul-searching, reflection, learning, and growing. It is an intentional and purposeful process, and so should parenting love. Unlearning toxic behaviors requires your deliberate effort to examine your past experiences and recognize your present emotions and triggers. As parents, we need space between our feelings and reactions to control our impulses. Caring and intentional love can help us create that space. When we know that our child misbehaves, not to give us a hard time, but because they're having a hard time, we might remember to keep loving them in tough parenting moments. If we remember we're our children's role models and protectors, maybe we can control our anger better. If we believe children are blessings from God, we may experience greater joy with them. All of these thoughts and feelings require our conscious and intentional effort.

Being physically affectionate with your child – even if it is the last thing you feel like doing when they are acting out, is an essential part of caring love. I like to pull my children in for a big hug and some deep breaths when they misbehave, allowing us to reconnect and re-center ourselves before we continue in a pattern of toxic behaviors on their end and mine. Caring love can also look like investing time into your child with one-on-one activities that allow them to connect with you on a deeper and more positive level. Other ways you can demonstrate caring love include:

- Writing notes (you can slip these in their lunch boxes or backpacks)

- Sharing a journal where you write letters back and forth

- Taking a timeout with your child in the heat of the moment

- Having regular check-ins where they can share what is going on with you

- Modeling the behavior you want to see

- Don't forget about non-verbal attunement; hugging your child, waiting for them to finish their stories, kind facial expressions, smiles, nods, winks, and gentle tone!

Is it difficult for you to forgive your child when they misbehave? Forgiving your child is a core component of caring love and something you need to learn well as a parent. Having perspective on the situation is vital, but how can you forgive your child for something they knew they were doing wrong? Maybe they lied to your face or ignored your agreements. The truth is that forgiving them is a choice you should make to continue to shore up and strengthen your relationship. This does not mean that there are no consequences for misbehavior. It just means that you are choosing to repair the relationship moving forward.

Loving your children does not always mean that you can't discipline them. It simply means that you are steering away from harsh discipline tactics that you may have used before. Take time to calm down before issuing discipline; you will have a clearer mind for your child's needs. Give them room to make mistakes so that they can learn, and allow natural consequences to take over.

When both the parent and the child are in good moods, expressing love is easy. The hard part is when either of them is distressed or upset. Because of the mutual parent-child interactions, negative feelings could diffuse from the parent to the child and vice versa. Imagine you're a loving and primarily peaceful parent. But a nagging and non-compliant child can still trigger you. So, how can you stay calm and loving in hard parenting moments? Think of your child's anger or non-compliance as a cry for help. They scream or lash out when overwhelmed and can't handle their emotions. An angry parent can never communicate empathically with an angry child. But a calm and attuned parent can. I've seen many angry children calmed down by affectionate parents. When one of my children is distressed, I offer a hug and give them some time to calm down. I try hard not to start by blaming, judging, or providing solutions. Instead, I try to make them feel secure and bring them peace. Only then we can communicate.

Be present and listen actively.

Parents who can become good listeners for their children do their families a big favor. This is not because they allocate time to hear their children. Listening is not the same as hearing. Listening is attentive and deliberate. It requires openness, mental and emotional presence, putting the distraction and biases aside, respect for the speaker, and sensing their feelings. One of the most common complaints by parents is that their children don't listen to them. If you expect your children to listen to you (and not just hear you!), have you reciprocated that?

If you're puzzled why your kids lie, lash out instead of asking for your help, or not telling you what bothers them, think about whether you have been a good listener for them. Parents and children are in two different worlds. They need a bridge to connect and mutually understand each other. Active listening by the parents acts like the columns for the communication bridge. If we lay a strong foundation and create a solid bridge, the flow of communication opens up. In simple terms, active listening creates an environment where children feel safe and free to speak up. Do you remember how your parents made you feel as a child? Maybe it was sometimes joyful and sometimes stressful. When did you enjoy listening to your parents more? To understand how your child feels under stress, imagine working with a self-centered manager who always likes to have his way. He never shows genuine interest in your thoughts and feelings, returning all communications to his opinions. How does it make you feel to communicate with him? I guess it's stressful and frustrating, and you wish you could avoid communication with him altogether. Unfortunately, children often don't listen to their parents because their parents' words and attitudes are stressful. Having a good communication bridge, which starts with the parents' active listening, prevents the build-up of stress.

We discussed the One-to-Ten rule in Chapter 3. Your child should get the opportunity to respond and explain ten times as much for every word you say. This rule is another embodiment of active listening, especially when giving advice. Parents feel the responsibility to guide and advise their children regularly. It's fair to teach your kids, but not before you actively listen to their stories (thoughts, feelings, problems, struggles, etc.). Parents should try to talk less, listen more, and let their children open up and talk more. Remember, if children can't speak up, they'll act up!

In my experience, the best way to implement the One-to-Ten rule is to avoid giving immediate advice or to fix the problem quickly. Instead, let the child speak and make them feel validated, heard, and seen by actively listening. An essential part of active listening is appreciating the speaker's feelings. This is especially the case with children. Attuned parents notice if their children are troubled and offer them the help and support they need.

Once you resist the temptation to teach your kids constantly, fix them, and be the lead actor in your parent-child play, there are some simple steps to develop an active listening habit. Here are a few examples:

- Be present and attentive: Eliminate distractions, listen carefully to your child's words, and give them your full attention. Don't try to multi-task while talking to your child; it can make them feel unimportant.

- Show empathy and be open-minded: Try to understand their perspective and respond compassionately. Be willing to learn from your child and consider their opinions and feelings.

- Don't interrupt or get defensive: Allow your child to complete their thoughts and avoid talking over them. Instead, listen objectively and try to understand their point of view, even if you disagree.

Show appreciation and acknowledge positive behaviors.

Parents can easily get swept away in their child's negative behaviors, but it is more helpful to both you and your child if you can take the time to focus on the positive behaviors instead. For example, one of my foster daughters struggled in school for quite some time. She used to get upset quickly, could not take no for an answer, and could not communicate well with her teacher or classmates. I was dealing with her situation daily, and it felt like all we did was complain about her poor behavior. I felt hopeless and powerless. However, the turning point came when I started to notice the things she did well and point them out to her as she was doing them. Gradually, her confidence grew, and those issues in the classroom became a thing of the past.

Catching my children doing something right and praise them for it is one of my favorite parenting hacks. Appreciating your child leads to better behavior and improved self-esteem. When you notice your child doing something good or correct, tell them right away. Then, you reinforce their positive behaviors by praising what they do or how they do something. You don't necessarily have to issue a reward for everything they do. Sometimes, a simple word of encouragement is all they need to know they are doing a great job. Here are a few examples of daily praise for your child:

- You're so talented!

- I can't get over how great you did at that activity!

- You should be proud of yourself for how well you've done!

- You're a great listener!

- You make me smile!

- I see how hard you tried to get that right!

- I can tell how hard you worked to make that happen!

- I knew you had it in you to finish your chores!

- Thank you for helping me around the house!

- You really earned my respect!

However, issuing descriptive praise to your child may be more effective. This details exactly what it is that you like about their behavior. For example: "I love that you found something quiet to do while I took that important work phone call. Thank you!" It details exactly what they did well and is more specific than general praise such as "you're a great kid." While both have a place when it comes to parenting from a place of caring love, descriptive praise often has a more powerful effect on how your child will respond to you. Too much praise can ring empty to your child's ears, as can unspecific praise. This is why descriptive praise is so much more effective. It has a place because it only praises the child for specific actions that they have done. You don't have to praise everything that your child does for them to know that they are caringly loved, but try to notice the things that make the difference in your child's life – areas where they might struggle the most, activities that they feel inadequate in, as well as areas where they shine.

There are many other ways to appreciate your child's efforts and achievements. Here are some examples:

- Physical affection, such as hugs, high-fives, or pats on the back.

- Offering incentives for good behavior, like special privileges or treats.

- Spending quality time reading a book together or playing a game.

- Encouraging independence by giving your child opportunities to take on responsibilities and make decisions independently.

Acknowledging your children's positive behaviors can build their self-esteem and foster a healthy, supportive relationship.

Be flexible and willing to adapt.

In Chapter 1, we reviewed various parenting styles, such as authoritarian, permissive, and authoritative. When you ask your child to do something just because "You are the dad (or mom)", you are being authoritarian. Such parents enforce their parenting rigidly and show little or no flexibility or consideration for the child. The opposite of authoritarian parenting is permissive parenting. Here, the child can choose, and the parent behaves like their best friend. Such a parent-child relationship could be very nurturing, but it lacks boundaries and fails to teach the child that every choice comes with inevitable consequences. We can place authoritarian and permissive parenting on the two opposite sides of the flexibility spectrum. Authoritative parenting is what most psychologists consider to be the sweet spot. It strikes a good balance between setting boundaries and consequences and offering the child a safe and warm environment. For example, you are authoritarian if you set a rule and ask your child to obey it, no questions asked. But if you discuss the same rule with your child, explain why you put it, let your child express their ideas, and be flexible enough to let go of the rule if needed, you are an authoritative parent. This kind of parenting is like the backbone; firm but flexible. That's why some people call it "backbone parenting."

Parenting flexibility does not mean giving in to children's demands. Instead, it refers to the psychological flexibility and adaptiveness to remain attuned and engaged with your kids daily and as they grow. It is the opposite of a black-and-white parenting approach, unwilling to change, adapt, compromise, or let go if needed. If you expect your child to behave in specific ways all the time and no matter what, you can highly benefit from some parenting flexibility. Parents and children change over extended time frames and experience varying moods and feelings in short periods. So, it is unrealistic to think that fixed approaches will always work (even if they sometimes work perfectly). Flexibility and adaptability are essential skills for parents to stay attuned to their children. They support their distressed children, ignore them when they act up, and oppose them firmly when they cross boundaries. Attuned parents move with their children's feelings and behaviors like a boat surfing on the waves. The challenging part about staying attuned to your child is that it can take tremendous mental, emotional, and sometimes physical energy. Being a constantly attuned parent is tough unless you're blessed with easy-going and good-tempered kids. Hence, you should make it easier for yourself to stay attuned at least for some time every day and in crucial moments by getting help, benefiting childcare services, taking care of yourself, and recharging physically and emotionally as much as possible.

There are many practical steps to strike a good balance between being firm and flexible. Here are some examples:

- Allow your kids second chances: Children make mistakes in their learning process. So instead of punishing them for every mistake, try to focus on teaching appropriate behavior and problem-solving skills.

- Stay open-minded: Consider alternative perspectives and be willing to try new things.

- Encourage exploration: Allow your child to try new activities, hobbies, or interests, even if they are different from your own.

- Allowing for independence: Give your child

space to make their own decisions and mistakes.

- Be responsive to change: Be flexible in your plans and routines, and be willing to adjust when necessary. You can stay committed to your parenting beliefs but adopt flexible approaches.

- Offer choices: Give your child options and allow them to make their own decisions within reason.

- Listen to their points of view and allow them to make meaningful contributions to decision-making. This can create a sense of responsibility, self-efficacy, and confidence in children.

Overall, being flexible and adaptable with children can help to build trust, strengthen the parent-child bond, and create a safe and secure environment for children to grow and develop. Remember that parenting is a learning process, and making mistakes is okay. The important thing is to recognize the mistakes, apologize and make a conscious effort to improve.

Use positive parenting practices.

Positive parenting is an excellent antidote to toxic parenting. It tries to satisfy a child's need for attention and power via positive interactions, i.e., by connecting with the child, recognizing their good behaviors, and nurturing them. When you address your children's need for attention and power regularly and positively, you minimize the instances in which they try to fulfill their emotional needs by misbehaving. Positive parenting proponents consider misbehavior a sign and not a problem or issue. Misbehavior is a cry for help; it's the child's way of saying something is wrong. The misbehavior will be largely gone if you meet their emotional needs for belonging and significance. This focus on basic human needs makes positive parenting valuable for all families.

One of the most important items in the positive parenting toolbox is behavior modification using reinforcement techniques. Reinforcement could be both positive and negative. Positive reinforcement encourages good behavior you wish to see more often. It amplifies what is already good and taps into your child's strengths and interests, increasing the odds of responding positively in the future. For example, one of my foster sons used to scream for minutes on end when it was time to do homework. At first, I started by taking away privileges, but I quickly learned that this only worsened the situation. So, instead, I rewarded him when he finished his homework. It made all the difference in his self-esteem and our budding relationship. Negative reinforcement is removing an aversive stimulus. So, "positive" or "negative" does not refer to the quality of the reinforcers. Instead, both reinforcers reward the operant, i.e., the person who exhibits a specific behavior. Positive reinforcement increases the frequency and probability of desired behaviors by adding an external and pleasant stimulus after exhibiting that behavior. In the case of negative reinforcement, the goal is to suppress behavior by removing an external but unpleasant stimulus once that behavior is stopped.

You use a positive reinforcer when you reward your child with a piece of cake when they clean their room. Negative reinforcement is the reinforcement of the desired behavior by removing an aversive stimulus. For example, the constant beeping sound you hear when you sit in your car and don't wear a seat belt is an excellent and annoying instance of negative reinforcement. Correct execution is vital for negative reinforcement to work. Unfortunately, many parents mix up negative reinforcement with punishment. While they intend to reinforce a behavior negatively, they punish their child and miss the reinforcement aspect altogether. Punishment is similar to reinforcement; since it could include adding or removing a stimulus.

The key here is to understand that reinforcement, whether positive or negative, is to strengthen a behavior. In contrast, punishment is to weaken a particular behavior. So, for example, a teacher can eliminate the homework if students work hard in class and get good grades (negative reinforcement by removing an undesirable stimulus, i.e., the homework). But on the other hand, the teacher can also give more homework if the students get poor grades (positive punishment by adding an undesirable stimulus, i.e., more homework). So, remember that reinforcement is to strengthen good behavior and is fundamentally different than punishment. I have covered positive parenting in detail in my other book, *Positive Parenting for the Explosive Child*.

Closing Remarks

The central theme of this book was parenting starts with you! If you are not at peace with yourself and cannot regulate your emotions, it will be tough (if not impossible) to model good behaviors for your child. Therefore, this book focused more on you (the parent) than your child. We started with recognizing toxic parenting traits, intergenerational cycles, and how toxic parents are created. The common feature of all toxic parents is emotional immaturity, which depicts itself in various forms, creating different types of toxic parents such as emotionally unstable, perfectionist, or disengaged. Our childhood experiences affect us profoundly and sometimes unconsciously. The coping skills and behavior patterns we learn in our formative years become deeply entrenched. We tend to repeat them because they feel familiar, and we know how to deal with them. We might even think we can gain mastery over them if we try them again; it might be different this time!

Chapter 2 answered questions such as why do parents become toxic? Are they born with toxicity, or do they turn toxic? Where does the toxin come from? Why do we repeat the same behaviors we despised in our parents? We discussed the epigenetic mechanisms and how certain events may turn our genes on, making it more likely to exhibit a specific behavior. We tend to repeat toxic parenting behaviors because they feel familiar and normal, and it's hard to change. As a result, we pass our childhood experiences down, even if we know they are unhealthy and hurtful. This cycle continues until we resolve the underlying trauma, change how we perceive and interpret our childhood experiences, learn new coping skills, and build new habits. The main takeaway was that we can't change our genes. But we can certainly influence our epigenetics. We can't change the past. But we can indeed perceive our past experiences in fresh and different ways.

Our childhood experiences are vital to our parenting styles and habits. Parents with unresolved childhood experiences are vulnerable to reacting based on their inner pain when stressed. Their children do or say something, they get triggered and react to relieve their emotional discomfort, even if the reaction is not in their children's interest. Over time, this vicious cycle occurs and calcifies into toxic parenting habits. Chapter 3 was about parenting detox by unlearning these toxic parenting habits. Toxic parenting is usually the outcome of a negative intergenerational cycle. Hence, you should break this cycle to stop being a toxic parent. Self-reflection about your current behaviors, childhood experiences, and family history is the cornerstone of this emotional cleansing. We tried to unweave the tangled web of toxicity by revisiting your parental beliefs, recognizing your triggers, and connecting before correcting.

Your children aren't giving you a hard time. They are having a hard time navigating their emotional experiences, and they look up to you for a role model, whether you want to be or not! When you have yours under control, you teach them a valuable lesson on how to manage theirs. Chapter 4 focused on emotional regulation to help you become more mindful of your parenting reactions, especially when you're tired, stressed out, or in a hurry. We reviewed various tips to become a more proactive parent to create a space between the stimuli and responses, giving yourself the headspace to consciously process and regulate feelings, control impulses, and respond rather than react.

One of the most common reasons for toxic parenting behaviors is acting based on our unfiltered personality traits instead of what is best for our children. For example, if your personality is decisive, willful, and authoritative, you may have a more strict approach to parenting and fall victim to toxic parenting behaviors, such as being overly critical and rigid. On the other hand, you might be a very nurturing parent who is susceptible to being overly controlling and trying to "fix" your children with extreme care. In Chapter 5, we reviewed the Five-Factor Model

(OCEAN), MBTI, and Enneagram personality tests to understand your personality better and find a parenting style that works for you. These tests provide unique insights into your psychological makeup and the motivations behind your parenting decisions. Each personality type has specific positive attributes to make wise and caring parents and some weaknesses. The personality tests show our intuitive and automatic mechanisms to interact with the world around us, including our children. As a result, we can recognize our weak spots and approach parenting with empathy, flexibility, self-reflection, and willingness to grow while prioritizing the well-being of our children.

Chapter 6 discussed the concept of bidirectional parenting and how it affects parent-child interactions. The child's characteristics could evoke different parenting behaviors, impacting the child, causing specific parenting reactions, and this circle continues! The central theme of Chapter 6 was parenting while staying attuned to your child. You are the adult, the role model, and ultimately accountable for responding maturely to your children. You can help them by staying attuned, recognizing their feelings, putting yourself in their shoes, listening actively, and offering caring love and support. If you stay attuned, the parenting journey will become less stressful and, hopefully, more enjoyable. We reviewed seven general guidelines to help you stay attuned to your child, act as their advocate, be more mindful, and never get toxic again. The common thread in these guidelines is to parent in such a way that you make fewer mistakes and, even more importantly, recover faster and easier from the parenting mistakes you'll inevitably make.

After many years of trial and error, I've realized that instead of looking for blueprints and exact recipes for parenting success, we better keep some general principles in mind to handle difficult parenting situations. These principles should be simple enough to remember in challenging moments and detailed enough to be actionable. They act like a compass to show the general direction; the exact route will depend on the unique hurdles along the way. I hope this book can serve as the compass in your parenting journey!

You can heal old wounds, recognize your triggers, break harmful parenting habits, and transform your childhood experiences into a driving force to raise your child with love without giving them the same traumas. If you enjoyed reading this book, please take a few moments and leave a review on Amazon to help future readers. Also, you might find my other book Positive Parenting for the Explosive Child interesting and valuable. In this book, you will discover how to practice positive parenting, focusing on raising explosive and easily-frustrated children. Parents who use positive parenting techniques still make mistakes. But they can survive their blunders, bounce back, and keep going because they proactively build a strong relationship with their child. So, give positive parenting a shot if you seek mutual respect and wish to enjoy yell-free parenting. Thank you, and good luck!

References

Introduction

S. (2022, October 18). National Parent Survey Overview and Key Insights. ZERO TO THREE. https://www.zerotothree.org/resource/national-parent-survey-overview-and-key-insights/

Gibson, L. C. (2015). Adult children of emotionally immature parents: How to heal from distant, rejecting, or self-involved parents. New Harbinger Publications, Inc.

Forward, S., & Buck, C. (2002). Toxic parents: Overcoming their hurtful legacy and reclaiming your life. Bantam Books.

Siegel, D. J., & Hartzell, M. (2013). Parenting from the inside out: How a deeper self-understanding can help you raise children who thrive. TarcherPerigee.

Markham, L. (2012). Peaceful parent, happy kids: How to stop yelling and start connecting. TarcherPerigee.

Miller, A., Hannum, H., & Hannum, H. (2002). For your own good: Hidden cruelty in child-rearing and the roots of violence. Farrar, Straus, Giroux.

Chapter One

Bailey, J. A., Hill, K. G., Oesterle, S., & Hawkins, J. D. (2009). Parenting practices and problem behavior across three generations: monitoring, harsh discipline, and drug use in the intergenerational transmission of externalizing behavior. Developmental psychology, 45 (5) 1214–1226.

Brent, D. J. (2018), Are we destined to repeat the mistakes our parents made?. CBC news. Retrieved June 15, 2022, from https://www.cbc.ca/parents/learning/view/are-we-destined-to-repeat-the-mistakes-our-parents-made

Clark, B., & Kurylo, B. Children benefit if they know about their relatives, study finds. Retrieved June 15, 2022, from http://shared.web.emory.edu/emory/news/releases/2010/03/children-benefit-if-they-know-about-their-relatives-study-finds.html#.YpYpmS-B1hC

Collins, L. M. (2019, June 30).How Lousy Parenting Can be Passed to the Next Generation. Deseret News. Retrieved June 15, 2022, from https://www.deseret.com/2016/5/6/20587945/how-lousy-parenting-can-be-passed-on-to-the-next-generation?_amp=true

Course Hero. Genetics and Behavior. Boundless Psychology. Retrieved June 15, 2022,

from https://www.coursehero.com/study-guides/bou
ndless-psychology/genetics-and-behavior/

Diener, E., & Lucas, R. E. Personality traits. Noba.
Retrieved June 15, 2022, from https://nobaproject.co
m/modules/personality-traits

Diener, E., Lucas, R. E., & Cummings, J.
A. (2019, June 28).Personality Traits. Introduction to Psychology. Retrieved June 15, 2022,
from https://openpress.usask.ca/introductiontopsych
ology/chapter/personality-traits/

Encyclopædia Britannica, incHeredity. Encyclopædia
Britannica. Retrieved June 15, 2022, from https://ww
w.britannica.com/science/heredity-genetics

Fox, M. (2016, July 13). Poor Parenting Can Be Passed
from Generation to Generation: Study. NBCNews.co
m. Retrieved June 15, 2022, from https://www.nbcne
ws.com/news/amp/ncna566036

Genes and Genetics Explained. Better
Health Channel. Retrieved June 15, 2022,
from https://www.betterhealth.vic.gov.au/health/cond
itionsandtreatments/genes-and-genetics

Jaehnig, J. (2022, March 31). What is inherited behavior? BetterHelp. Retrieved June 15, 2022,
from https://www.betterhelp.com/advice/behavior/w
hat-is-inherited-behavior/

Management Study Guide. Personality Traits: Meaning and Different Types of Traits. Retrieved June 15,
2022, from https://www.managementstudyguide.com
/personality-traits.htm

Morris, H. 6 benefits of knowing your family history - story terrace. Retrieved June 15, 2022, from https://blog.storyterrace.com/uk/6-benefits-of-knowing-your-family-history

National University. (2021, June 30). Is human behavior genetic or learned? Retrieved June 15, 2022, from https://www.nu.edu/resources/ask-an-expert-is-human-behavior-genetic-or-learned/amp/

Philpott, M. L. (2021, October 24).Learning from Our Mistakes, for Our Kids and Ourselves. The Washington Post. Retrieved June 15, 2022, from https://www.washingtonpost.com/news/parenting/wp/2017/01/17/learning-from-our-mistakes-for-kids-and-ourselves/

The Public Engagement team at the Wellcome Genome Campus. (2021, July 21). What is inheritance? Retrieved June 15, 2022, from https://www.yourgenome.org/facts/what-is-inheritance

Szczypinski, S. (2021, October 24). Abusive Parenting Styles Can Be Inherited. The Washington Post. Retrieved   June   15,   2022,   from https://www.washingtonpost.com/news/parenting/wp/2018/05/04/abusive-parenting-styles-can-be-inherited-heres-are-5-ways-to-break-the-cycle/

U.S. National Library of Medicine. (n.d.). Why is it important to know my family health history?: Medlineplus Genetics. MedlinePlus. Retrieved June 15, 2022, from https://medlineplus.gov/genetics/understanding/inheritance/familyhistory/

Wagner, C. (2020, March 8). 7 Ways We Repeat the Mistakes Our Parents Made. SchoolMyKids. Retrieved June 15, 2022, from https://www.schoolmykids.com/parenting/ways -we-repeat-the-mistakes-our-parents-made

Wardleigh, C. (n.d.). 5 Benefits of Knowing Your Family History. Select Health. Retrieved June 15, 2022, from https://selecthealth.org/blog/2019/08/5-benefits -of-knowing-your-family-history

Why We Need Family History More Now than Ever. FamilySearch. (2021, December 15). Retrieved June 15, 2022, from https://www.familysearch.org/en/blog/wh y-we-need-family-history-now-more-than-ever

Gibson, L. C. (2015). Adult children of emotionally immature parents: How to heal from distant, rejecting, or self-involved parents. New Harbinger Publications, Inc.

Forward, S., & Buck, C. (2002). Toxic parents: Overcoming their hurtful legacy and reclaiming your life. Bantam Books.

Siegel, D. J., & Hartzell, M. (2013). Parenting from the inside out: How a deeper self-understanding can help you raise children who thrive. TarcherPerigee.

Markham, L. (2012). Peaceful parent, happy kids: How to stop yelling and start connecting. Tarcher-Perigee.

Miller, A., Hannum, H., & Hannum, H. (2002). For your own good: Hidden cruelty in child-rearing and the roots of violence. Farrar, Straus, Giroux.

Chapter Two

Boone, N. (2021, March 24). What is generational trauma and how can we heal from it? Ensemble Therapy. Retrieved June 15, 2022, from https://www.ensemblet herapy.com/blog/what-is-generational-trauma

Cooks-Campbell, A. (2022, February 2). What is transgenerational trauma, and how does it affect our families?BetterUp. Retrieved June 15, 2022, from https://www.betterup.com/blog/transgeneratio nal-trauma?hs_amp=true

Daniels, C. (2022, May 8). 3 tips to break toxic generational patterns now! Adorned H. Retrieved June 15,   2022,   from https://www.adornedheart.com/3-strategies-to-break-t he-chains-of-toxic-generational-patterns-curses-traumas /

Duke University. (n.d.). Inter-generational trauma: 6 ways it affects families. Office for Institutional Equity. Retrieved June 15, 2022, from https://oie.duke.edu/in ter-generational-trauma-6-ways-it-affects-families

Gillespie, C. (2020, October 27). Generational trauma might explain your anxiety and depression. Health. Retrieved June 15, 2022, from https://www.health.com/c ondition/ptsd/generational-trauma

How Gen Zers are breaking toxic cycles of trauma in their families. Mindpath Health. (2022, February 10). Retrieved   June   15,   2022,   from https://www.mindpath.com/resource/how-gen-zers-are -breaking-toxic-cycles-of-trauma-in-their-families/#:~:te xt=Studies%20show%20that%20exposure%20to,every%20aspect%20of%20their%20life.

Kelloway, R. (2022, April 11). How childhood trauma affects parenting styles. Life Care Wellness. Retrieved June 15, 2022, from https://life-care-wellness.com/how-childhood-trauma-affects-parenting-styles/

Lara, D. (2021, October 30). Breaking the cycle of dysfunctional generational patterns in families. Medium. Retrieved June 15, 2022, from https://medium.com/swlh/4-things-emotionally-mature-parents-dont-do-e68e2a24578c

Lehal, M. (2020, March 14). Breaking generational patterns: Developing healthy relationships. Wake Counseling & Mediation. Retrieved June 15, 2022, from https://www.wakecounseling.com/therapy-blog/developing-healthy-relationships

McClanahan, J. (2018, January 17). I grew up with family dysfunction, but this is how I'm breaking the cycle. Scary Mommy. Retrieved June 15, 2022, from https://www.scarymommy.com/breaking-cycle-family-dysfunction

Michael, J. (2019, September 2). Your generational legacy: How to break destructive patterns. Jody Michael Associates. Retrieved June 15, 2022, from https://www.jodymichael.com/blog/your-generational-legacy-how-to-break-destructive-patterns/

Sigal, J. J., Dinicola, V. F., & Buonvino, M. (1988). Grandchildren of Survivors: Can Negative Effects of Prolonged Exposure to Excessive Stress be Observed Two

Generations Later? The Canadian Journal of Psychiatry, 33(3), 207–212. https://doi.org/10.1177/0706743788 03300309

University of California - Los Angeles Health Sciences. (2018, July 9). Parents who had severe trauma, stresses in childhood more likely to have kids with behavioral health problems. ScienceDaily. Retrieved June 15, 2022 from www.sciencedaily.com/releases/2018/07/180709 101155.htm

Young, K. (2020, August 17). Breaking the cycle of toxic parenting - how to silence old toxic messages for good. Hey Sigmund. Retrieved June 15, 2022, from https://www.heysigmund.com/breaking-the-cycl e-of-toxic-parenting/

Lehrner, A., & Yehuda, R. (2018). Cultural trauma and epigenetic inheritance. Development and Psychopathology, 30(5), 1763–1777. https://doi.org/10.1 017/s0954579418001153

Yehuda, R., Daskalakis, N. P., Lehrner, A., Desarnaud, F., Bader, H. N., Makotkine, I., Flory, J. D., Bierer, L. M., & Meaney, M. J. (2014). Influences of maternal and paternal PTSD on epigenetic regulation of the glucocorticoid receptor gene in Holocaust survivor offspring. American Journal of Psychiatry, 171(8), 872–880. http s://doi.org/10.1176/appi.ajp.2014.13121571

Gibson, L. C. (2015). Adult children of emotionally immature parents: How to heal from distant, rejecting, or self-involved parents. New Harbinger Publications, Inc.

Forward, S., & Buck, C. (2002). Toxic parents: Overcoming their hurtful legacy and reclaiming your life. Bantam Books.

Siegel, D. J., & Hartzell, M. (2013). Parenting from the inside out: How a deeper self-understanding can help you raise children who thrive. TarcherPerigee.

Markham, L. (2012). Peaceful parent, happy kids: How to stop yelling and start connecting. TarcherPerigee.

Miller, A., Hannum, H., & Hannum, H. (2002). For your own good: Hidden cruelty in child-rearing and the roots of violence. Farrar, Straus, Giroux.

Chapter 3

10 signs you had toxic parents - and how to break the cycle. Fairygodboss. (n.d.). Retrieved June 23, 2022, from https://fairygodboss.com/articles/toxic-parents

5 most common behavioral issues. 5 Most Common Behavioral Issues : Greater Lowell Psychiatric Associates, LLC: Psychiatric & Mental Health Specialists. (n.d.). Retrieved June 23, 2022, from https://www.greaterlowellpsychassoc.com/blog/5-most-common-behavioral-issues

Ambardar, S. (2021, July 19). Narcissistic personality disorder. Practice Essentials, Background, Pathophysiology and Etiology. Retrieved June 29, 2022, from https://emedicine.medscape.com/article/151941 7-overview#a5

Arora, M. (2020, November 18). 16 signs of Bad Parenting & its impact on children. FirstCry Parenting. Retrieved June 23, 2022, from https://parenting.firstcry.com/articles/bad-parenting-signs-effects/

Ashley, S. (2021, May 16). 16 characteristics of highly toxic parents. Scary Mommy. Retrieved June 23, 2022, from https://www.scarymommy.com/16-characteristics-toxic-parents/amp

Behavioral disorder symptoms, causes and effects. PsychGuides.com. (n.d.). Retrieved June 23, 2022, from https://www.psychguides.com/behavioral-disorders/#:~:text=Putting%20blame%20on%20others,Having%20difficulty%20in%20handling%20frustration

Business Insider. (n.d.). 10 toxic things parents do that make children unhealthy adults. Business Insider. Retrieved June 23, 2022, from https://www.businessinsider.com/toxic-behaviors-parents-make-children-unhealthy-less-functional-adults?amp

Butler, C. (2021, April 21). 4 examples of toxic parenting and how to fix them. Quick and Dirty Tips. Retrieved June 23, 2022, from https://www.quickanddirtytips.com/parenting/behavior/4-examples-of-toxic-parenting-and-how-to-fix-them?amp

Champion, L. (2019, June 13). 9 signs you were raised in a toxic family (and how to move on). PureWow. Retrieved June 23, 2022, from https://www.purewow.com/wellness/toxic-family-signs

Cherry, K. (2021, May 29). Denial as a Defense Mechanism. Verywell Mind. Retrieved June 23, 2022,

from https://www.verywellmind.com/denial-as-a-defe
nse-mechanism-5114461

Child discipline. Verywell Family. (n.d.). Retrieved
June 23, 2022, from https://www.verywellfamily.com/
discipline-4157347

Cotto, T. (2020, July 18). 10 ways we pass on toxic behaviors to our children. Moms. Retrieved June 23,
2022, from https://www.moms.com/10-ways-parents
-pass-toxic-behaviors-children/amp/

Ducharme, J. (2018, June 5). Toxic relationships:
Signs, help and what to do. Time. Retrieved June 29,
2022, from https://time.com/5274206/toxic-relations
hip-signs-help/

Erickson, R. (2019, October 17). Parents' effect on
child behavior. Hello Motherhood. Retrieved June 23,
2022, from https://www.hellomotherhood.com/article
/75282-parents-effect-child-behavior/

Gilmerm. (2021, October 18). 7 signs of a toxic parent
and how to Cope. Cleveland Clinic. Retrieved June 23,
2022, from https://health.clevelandclinic.org/toxic-par
enting-traits/

Grohol, J. (2022, April 28). Examples of common
defense mechanisms. Psych Central. Retrieved June 23,
2022, from https://psychcentral.com/health/common
-defense-mechanisms

Higuera, V. (2019, September 20). Uninvolved parenting: Pros and cons, effects, examples, more. Healthline. Retrieved June 23, 2022, from https://www.healt
hline.com/health/parenting/uninvolved-parenting

Marcin, A. (2020, July 16). Understanding and dealing with toxic parents and co-parents. Healthline. Retrieved June 23, 2022, from https://www.healthline.com/health/parenting/toxic-parents#:~:text=%E2%80%9CToxic%20parent%E2%80%9D%20is%20an%20umbrella,to%20things%20that%20you%20need.

McQueen, J. (n.d.). Toxic parents: How to manage them. WebMD. Retrieved June 23, 2022, from https://www.webmd.com/sex-relationships/features/toxic-parents

Nguyen, T. P., Karney, B. R., & Bradbury, T. N. (2017). Childhood abuse and later marital outcomes: Do partner characteristics moderate the association?. Journal of family psychology : JFP : journal of the Division of Family Psychology of the American Psychological Association (Division 43), 31(1), 82–92. https://doi.org/10.1037/fam0000208

Nunez, J. L. O. (2022, February 15). Stop being a toxic parent. Medium. Retrieved June 23, 2022, from https://medium.com/better-advice/stop-being-a-toxic-parent-b742ea935f7

Raypole, C. (2022, January 19). 12 signs you might have narcissistic victim syndrome. Healthline. Retrieved June 23, 2022, from https://www.healthline.com/health/narcissistic-victim-syndrome

Seltzer, F. (2021, October 5). Here's what makes 'authoritative parents' different from the rest-and why psychologists say it's the best parenting style. CNBC.

Retrieved   June   29,   2022,   from
https://www.cnbc.com/2021/10/05/child-psychologist
-explains-why-authoritative-parenting-is-the-best-style-f
or-raising-smart-confident-kids.html

Shahida Arabi, M. A. (2017, August 21). 11 signs
youre the victim of narcissistic abuse. Psych Central.
Retrieved   June   23,   2022,   from
https://psychcentral.com/blog/recovering-narcissist/20
17/08/11-signs-youre-the-victim-of-narcissistic-abuse#1

Signs and symptoms of narcissistic abuse syndrome.
Rosglas Recovery. (2021, March 23). Retrieved June 23,
2022, from https://www.rosglasrecovery.com/signs-an
d-symptoms-of-narcissistic-abuse-syndrome/

Sussex Publishers. (n.d.). The narcissistic family
legacy. Psychology Today. Retrieved June 29, 2022, from
https://www.psychologytoday.com/us/blog/women-au
tism-spectrum-disorder/202005/the-narcissistic-family
-legacy

Szczypinski, S. (2021, October 24). Perspective |
abusive parenting styles can be inherited. here are 5 ways
to break the cycle. The Washington Post. Retrieved June
23,   2022,   from
https://www.washingtonpost.com/news/parenting/wp
/2018/05/04/abusive-parenting-styles-can-be-inherited
-heres-are-5-ways-to-break-the-cycle/

Thorpe, J. R., & Polish, J. (2022, April 1). 13 signs
you grew up with a toxic parent & didn't know it. Bustle.
Retrieved June 23, 2022, from https://www.bustle.com
/wellness/signs-you-grew-up-with-toxic-parent-experts

Ubaidi, A. (n.d.). Cost of growing up in dysfunctional family. ClinMed International Library. Retrieved June 23, 2022, from https://clinmedjournals.org/articles/jfmdp/journal-of-family-medicine-and-disease-prevention-jfmdp-3-059.php?jid=-

Warning signs of behavioral disorders. Discovery Mood & Anxiety Program. (2019, May 8). Retrieved June 23, 2022, from https://discoverymood.com/blog/warning-signs-behavioral-disorders/

Gibson, L. C. (2015). Adult children of emotionally immature parents: How to heal from distant, rejecting, or self-involved parents. New Harbinger Publications, Inc.

Forward, S., & Buck, C. (2002). Toxic parents: Overcoming their hurtful legacy and reclaiming your life. Bantam Books.

Siegel, D. J., & Hartzell, M. (2013). Parenting from the inside out: How a deeper self-understanding can help you raise children who thrive. TarcherPerigee.

Markham, L. (2012). Peaceful parent, happy kids: How to stop yelling and start connecting. TarcherPerigee.

Miller, A., Hannum, H., & Hannum, H. (2002). For your own good: Hidden cruelty in child-rearing and the roots of violence. Farrar, Straus, Giroux.

Chapter 4

Anger and anger management for parents. Raising Children Network. (2020, June 22). Retrieved June 23,

2022,   from
https://raisingchildren.net.au/guides/first-1000-days/lo
oking-after-yourself/anger-management-for-parents

Beurkens, N. (2021, December 8). Strategies to help parents manage emotions and their behavior. Nicole Beurkens. Retrieved June 23, 2022, from https://www.drbeurkens.com/podcast/strategies-to-help-parents-manage-emotions/

Controlling your anger as a parent. Pregnancy Birth and Baby. (n.d.). Retrieved June 23, 2022, from https://www.pregnancybirthbaby.org.au/amp/article/controlling-your-anger-as-a-parent

Controlling your anger as a parent. Pregnancy Birth and Baby. (n.d.). Retrieved June 23, 2022, from https://www.pregnancybirthbaby.org.au/amp/article/controlling-your-anger-as-a-parent

Gonzales, S. (2019, May 29). How children pick up on parents' anxiety and anger and why we should be mindful of how we act. South China Morning Post. Retrieved   June   23,   2022,   from https://www.scmp.com/lifestyle/health-wellness/article/3012143/how-children-pick-parents-anxiety-and-anger-and-why-we

Henter, R., & Nastasa, L. E. (1AD, January 1). Parents' emotion management for personal well-being when challenged by their online work and their children's online school. Frontiers. Retrieved June 23, 2022, from https://www.frontiersin.org/articles/10.3389/fpsyg.2021.751153/full

Hester, M. (2020, November 13). Kids pick up on parents' stress. Contemporary Pediatrics. Retrieved June 23, 2022, from https://www.contemporarypediatrics.com/view/kids-pick-parents-stress

Lambie, J. (2018, October 11). Should you hide negative emotions from children? The Conversation: In-depth analysis, research, news and ideas from leading academics and researchers. Retrieved June 23, 2022, from https://theconversation.com/amp/should-you-hide-negative-emotions-from-children-104710

Lerner, C. (n.d.). Managing your own emotions: The key to positive, effective parenting. ZERO TO THREE. Retrieved   June   23,   2022,   from https://www.zerotothree.org/resources/338-managing-your-own-emotions-the-key-to-positive-effective-parenting#:~:text=Learning%20to%20manage%20your%20own

Lucas, F. (2022, March 11).Angry parents are impacting children's brain development researchers say. The Sector. Retrieved June 29, 2022, from https://thesector.com.au/2021/03/25/angry-parents-are-impacting-childrens-brain-development-researchers-say/

Managing emotions: How parents show children how to behave. Kars4Kids Parenting. (2020, February 5). Retrieved June 23, 2022, from https://parenting.kars4kids.org/managing-emotions-how-parents-show-children-how-to-behave/amp/

Markham, L. (n.d.). How to handle your anger at your child. Psychology Today. Retrieved June 23, 2022, from https://www.psychologytoday.com/us/blog/peaceful-parents-happy-kids/201605/how-handle-your-anger-your-child?amp

Pincus, D. (2021, October 4). How to control your anger with kids. Empowering Parents. Retrieved June 23, 2022, from https://www.empoweringparents.com/article/calm-parenting-get-control-child-making-angry/

Schwarz, N. (2016, January 11). TIRED OF BEING AN ANGRY PARENT? 6 TIPS TO CONTROL YOUR ANGER. Imperfect Families. Retrieved June 23, 2022, from https://imperfectfamilies.com/tired-of-being-an-angry-parent-6-tips-to-control-your-anger/

Sharing your negative emotions with your kids is better than hiding them. Popular Science. (2021, April 26). Retrieved June 23, 2022, from https://www.popsci.com/parents-negative-emotions-children-sharing/?amp

Should you try to hide your negative emotions from your kids? Should You Try to Hide Your Negative Emotions from Your Kids? | Society for Personality and Social Psychology. (2017, January 12). Retrieved June 23, 2022, from https://spsp.org/news-center/character-context-blog/should-you-try-hide-your-negative-emotions-your-kids

Soderlund, A. (2021, October 18). 10 emotion-coaching phrases to use when your child is upsetAs. Nurture and Thrive. Retrieved June 23, 2022, from https://nurtureandthriveblog.com/emotion-coaching-parents/

Vassar, G. (2020, December 10). How does a parent's anger impact his or her child? Lakeside. Retrieved June 23, 2022, from https://lakesidelink.com/blog/lakeside/how-does-a-parents-anger-impact-his-or-her-child/

Waters SF, Karnilowicz HR, West TV, Mendes WB. Keep it to yourself? Parent emotion suppression influences physiological linkage and interaction behavior.J Fam Psychol.April 23, 2020. Epub ahead of print. doi: 10.1037/fam0000664.

Le, B. M., & Impett, E. A. (2016). The costs of suppressing negative emotions and amplifying positive emotions during parental caregiving.Personality and Social Psychology Bulletin, 42(3), 323–336.

Gibson, L. C. (2015). Adult children of emotionally immature parents: How to heal from distant, rejecting, or self-involved parents. New Harbinger Publications, Inc.

Forward, S., & Buck, C. (2002). Toxic parents: Overcoming their hurtful legacy and reclaiming your life. Bantam Books.

Siegel, D. J., & Hartzell, M. (2013). Parenting from the inside out: How a deeper self-understanding can help you raise children who thrive. Tarcher Perigee.

Markham, L. (2012). Peaceful parent, happy kids: How to stop yelling and start connecting. Tarcher Perigee.

Miller, A., Hannum, H., & Hannum, H. (2002). For your own good: Hidden cruelty in child-rearing and the roots of violence. Farrar, Straus, Giroux.

Chapter 5

The Children's Hospital of Philadelphia. (2019, January 24). The do's and don'ts of disciplining your child. Children's Hospital of Philadelphia. Retrieved June 23, 2022, from https://www.chop.edu/news/health-tip/dos-and-donts-disciplining-your-child

Denise, J. (2021, October 9). How can we break toxic parenting cycles and raise emotionally healthy kids? MadameNoire. Retrieved June 23, 2022, from https://madamenoire.com/1137571/how-can-we-break-toxic-parenting-cycles-and-raise-emotionally-healthy-kids/amp/

Dilip, M. (2022, March 23). Parenting strengths and weaknesses: How to develop effective parenting skills. ParentCircle. Retrieved June 23, 2022, from https://www.parentcircle.com/parenting-strengths-and-weaknesses-how-to-develop-effective-parenting-skills/article

How to discipline your child the smart and Healthy Way. UNICEF Parenting. (n.d.). Retrieved June 23, 2022, from https://www.unicef.org/parenting/child-care/how-discipline-your-child-smart-and-healthy-way

How to unlearn toxic behaviors that hold you back. Discover GR8NESS. (2020, February 25). Retrieved June 23, 2022, from https://www.gr8ness.com/unlearning-toxic-behaviors/amp/

Iannelli, V. (2022, June 19). 11 Common Parenting Mistakes to Avoid. Verywell Family. Retrieved June 23,

2022, from https://www.verywellfamily.com/common
-parenting-mistakes-2633998

Kadane, L. (2019, December 19). Kick your bad parenting habits in 2020. Stuck in a rut: How to kick your
bad parenting habits in 2020. Retrieved June 23, 2022,
from https://www.todaysparent.com/family/parenting
/how-to-get-out-of-a-parenting-rut/amp/

Khan, A. (2020, August 24). 10 most
common parenting issues and their solutions.
FirstCry Parenting. Retrieved June 23, 2022,
from https://parenting.firstcry.com/articles/10-comm
on-parenting-issues-and-their-solutions/?amp

Lee, K. (2021, July 5). How to reprimand
your child the right way (and mistakes to
avoid). Verywell Family. Retrieved June 23, 2022,
from https://www.verywellfamily.com/the-9-biggest-d
iscipline-mistakes-parents-make-620112

Lindberg, S. (2020, September 25). Bad parenting:
Signs, effects, and how to change it. Healthline. Retrieved
June 23, 2022, from https://www.healthline.com/heal
th/parenting/bad-parenting

Pietroforte, M. (2022, May 4). 5 toxic behaviors & how to unlearn them. Company Culture Tips. Retrieved June 23, 2022,
from https://blog.deliveringhappiness.com/5-toxic-wo
rkplace-behaviors-how-to-unlearn-them?hs_amp=true

Saying 'no' to friends isn't selfish-here's why. The
Everygirl. (2019, October 11). Retrieved June 23, 2022,

from https://theeverygirl.com/why-saying-no-isnt-selfish/

The Nemours Foundation. (n.d.). Nine steps to more effective parenting (for parents) - nemours kidshealth. KidsHealth. Retrieved June 29, 2022, from https://kidshealth.org/en/parents/nine-steps.html

Thomas. (2022, February 21). 10 simple steps to stop toxic parenting. The Good Men Project. Retrieved June 23, 2022, from https://goodmenproject.com/ethics-values/10-simple-steps-stop-toxic-parenting-fiff/

Young, K. (2020, August 17). Breaking the cycle of toxic parenting - how to silence old toxic messages for goodw. Hey Sigmund. Retrieved June 23, 2022, from https://www.heysigmund.com/breaking-the-cycle-of-toxic-parenting/

Zorn, A. (2022, February 3). The day I realized I was bullying my kids - and how I got out of the yelling cycle. Bounceback Parenting. Retrieved June 23, 2022, from https://bouncebackparenting.com/the-day-i-realized-i-was-bullying-my-kids/

Gibson, L. C. (2015). Adult children of emotionally immature parents: How to heal from distant, rejecting, or self-involved parents. New Harbinger Publications, Inc.

Forward, S., & Buck, C. (2002). Toxic parents: Overcoming their hurtful legacy and reclaiming your life. Bantam Books.

Siegel, D. J., & Hartzell, M. (2013). Parenting from the inside out: How a deeper self-understanding can help you raise children who thrive. TarcherPerigee.

Markham, L. (2012). Peaceful parent, happy kids: How to stop yelling and start connecting. Tarcher-Perigee.

Miller, A., Hannum, H., & Hannum, H. (2002). For your own good: Hidden cruelty in child-rearing and the roots of violence. Farrar, Straus, Giroux.

Chapter 6

Acknowledging your achievements is a form of self-care. Harvard Business Review. (2017, November 23). Retrieved June 24, 2022, from https://hbr.org/tip/2017/11/acknowledging-your-achievements-is-a-form-of-self-care

Polderman, T., Benyamin, B., de Leeuw, C. et al. Meta-analysis of the heritability of human traits based on fifty years of twin studies. Nat Genet 47, 702–709 (2015). https://doi.org/10.1038/ng.3285.

Lansford, J. E., et. al. (2018). Bidirectional Relations Between Parenting and Behavior Problems From Age 8 to 13 in Nine Countries. Journal of Research on Adolescence, 28(3), 571–590. https://doi.org/10.1111/jora.12381

Hogenboom, M. (n.d.). Do children change our behaviour? BBC Future. https://www.bbc.com/future/article/20220104-how-parenting-changes-you

Booth, J. (2022, December 20). 9 Enneagram Personality Types: Strengths, Weaknesses And More. Forbes

Health. https://www.forbes.com/health/mind/enneag
ram-types/

Cron, I. M. (2022). The Story of You: An Enneagram Journey to Becoming Your True Self. Harper One.

Brown, J. (2021, October 26). How to teach yourself to be (a little bit) more optimistic. Fatherly. Retrieved June 24, 2022, from https://www.fatherly.com/love-m oney/how-to-be-more-optimistic/amp

Casares, W. (n.d.). Importance of self-care: Why parents need time out to recharge. HealthyChildren.org. Retrieved   June   24,   2022,   from https://www.healthychildren.org/English/family-life/fa mily-dynamics/Pages/Importance-of-Self-Care.aspx

Chillcoat, S. (2019, June 8). Self-credit: How to appre-ciate progress and reward yourself. Sam Chillcott Coach-ing. Retrieved June 24, 2022, from https://www.samch illcott.com/self-credit/

Clear, J. (2018, November 13). How to start new habits that actually stick. James Clear. Retrieved June 24, 2022, from https://jamesclear.com/three-steps-habit-c hange

Clear, J. (2020, February 4). How to build a new habit: This is your strategy guide. James Clear. Retrieved June 24, 2022, from https://jamesclear.com/habit-guide

Davenport, B. (2022, May 19). 25 good character traits list essential for happiness. Live Bold and Bloom. Re-trieved June 24, 2022, from https://liveboldandbloom. com/10/relationships/good-character-traits

Elston, C. (2018, April 24). The power of optimism and positive parenting in practice. L.A. Parent. Retrieved June 24, 2022, from https://www.laparent.com/the-po wer-of-optimism-positive-parenting/

Resilience - American Psychological Association (APA). (n.d.). Retrieved June 24, 2022, from https://w ww.apa.org/topics/resilience/

Scott, E. (2019, November 19). 9 ways to be more resilient in the face of stress. Verywell Mind. Retrieved June 24, 2022, from https://www.verywellmind.com/c ope-with-stress-and-become-more-resilient-3144889

Steber, C. (2016, April 15). 11 tips for being a bit more friendly in everyday life. Bustle. Retrieved June 24, 2022, from https://www.bustle.com/articles/154954-11-tips -for-being-a-bit-more-friendly-in-everyday-life

U.S. Department of Health and Human Services. (n.d.). 7 steps to manage stress and build resilience. National Institutes of Health. Retrieved June 24, 2022, f   r   o   m https://orwh.od.nih.gov/in-the-spotlight/all-articles/7-s teps-manage-stress-and-build-resilience#:~:text=Start%2 0with%20small%20changes%20in

Kaitlin Woolley, Ayelet Fishbach, For the Fun of It: Harnessing Immediate Rewards to Increase Persistence in Long-Term Goals, Journal of Consumer Research, Volume 42, Issue 6, April 2016, Pages 952–966, https ://doi.org/10.1093/jcr/ucv098

Gibson, L. C. (2015). Adult children of emotionally immature parents: How to heal from distant, rejecting, or self-involved parents. New Harbinger Publications, Inc.

Forward, S., & Buck, C. (2002). Toxic parents: Overcoming their hurtful legacy and reclaiming your life. Bantam Books.

Siegel, D. J., & Hartzell, M. (2013). Parenting from the inside out: How a deeper self-understanding can help you raise children who thrive. TarcherPerigee.

Markham, L. (2012). Peaceful parent, happy kids: How to stop yelling and start connecting. TarcherPerigee.

Miller, A., Hannum, H., & Hannum, H. (2002). For your own good: Hidden cruelty in child-rearing and the roots of violence. Farrar, Straus, Giroux.

5 benefits of Parental Love. Focus on the Family. (2022, April 1). Retrieved June 24, 2022, from https://www.focusonthefamily.com/parenting/parental-love/

5 easy strategies to help your child overcome weakness. mamawearpapashirt. (2021, July 8). Retrieved June 24, 2022, from http://www.mamawearpapashirt.com/2017/05/help-your-child-overcome-weakness-5-easy-tips/

Bell, V. (2022, March 21). What does radical love look like? Awana. Retrieved June 24, 2022, from https://www.awana.org/2019/02/20/radical-love-look-like/

Douglas, E. (2021, March 10). Parenting as a radical act of love. The Nation. Retrieved June 24, 2022, from https://www.thenation.com/radical-parenting/

Dulong, J. (2021, December 7). Kindness begins at home: How Traci Baxley uses 'radical love' to conquer fear and promote justice. ABC17NEWS. Retrieved June 24, 2022, from https://abc17news.com/news/2021/12/07/kindness-begins-at-home-how-traci-baxley-uses-radical-love-to-conquer-fear-and-promote-justice/

Ganesh, A. (2021, July 26). The Art of Forgiveness. When Parents Forgive, Children Learn As Well; How Children Learn Forgiveness. Retrieved June 24, 2022, from https://www.parentcircle.com/why-does-forgiveness-matter-for-parents/article

Huerta, D. (2022, April 1). Demonstrating steadfast love in parenting. Focus on the Family. Retrieved June 24, 2022, from https://www.focusonthefamily.com/parenting/demonstrating-steadfast-love-in-parenting/

Lindberg, S. (2020, September 25). Bad parenting: Signs, effects, and how to change it. Healthline. Retrieved June 24, 2022, from https://www.healthline.com/health/parenting/bad-parenting

Little scholars. (n.d.). Retrieved June 24, 2022, from https://www.littlescholarsllc.com/resources/100-ways-to-praise-your-child/

Luce, K. (2014, March 1). Love your kids. leave them alone: The art of radical parenting. ~ Kristin S. Luce: Elephant Journal. Retrieved June 24, 2022, from https://www.elephantjournal.com/2013/12/love-your-kids-leave-them-alone-the-art-of-radical-parenting-kristin-s-luce/

Meyers, M. K. (2017, March 3). How to effectively praise your child (hint: "you're amazing!"

is harmful). WeHaveKids. Retrieved June 24, 2022, from https://wehavekids.com/parenting/52-Ways-to-Praise-Your-Child-Without-Saying-Youre-Amazing

The Nemours Foundation. (n.d.). Nine steps to more effective parenting (for parents) - norton children's. KidsHealth. Retrieved June 24, 2022, from https://kidshealth.org/NortonChildrens/en/parents/nine-steps.html

Praise, encouragement and rewards. Raising Children Network. (2020, August 31). Retrieved June 24, 2022, from https://raisingchildren.net.au/toddlers/connecting-communicating/connecting/praise

Rules of parenting. The rules of parenting - for loving and caring parents. (n.d.). Retrieved June 24, 2022, from http://www.rulesofparenting.com/forgive-and-forget-5-tips-on-forgiving-a-child-who-hurts-you/

Walker, D. B. (2018, March 8). How to destroy a child: Make them feel rejected and unloved. Medium. Retrieved June 24, 2022, from https://medium.com/@williamfwalkerjr/how-to-destroy-a-child-make-them-feel-rejected-and-unloved-95b89fcdff1c

Walker, T. (2021, June 15). You should forgive your kids. Parent Cue. Retrieved June 24, 2022, from https://theparentcue.org/you-should-forgive-your-kids/

What is Radical Love? One Tree Center. (2016, December 31). Retrieved June 24, 2022, from https://onetreecenter.org/what-is-radical-love/

Yates, S. (2018, May 11). Helping your kids understand strengths and weaknesses.

MomLife Today. Retrieved June 24, 2022, from https://momlifetoday.com/2012/03/helping-your-kids-understand-strengths-and-weaknesses/

Gottman Institute. (2021, February 3). Mindful parenting: How to respond instead of react. The Gottman Institute. Retrieved June 24, 2022, from https://www.gottman.com/blog/mindful-parenting-how-to-respond-instead-of-react/

Li, P. (2022, June 20). Top 10 good parenting tips - best advice. Parenting For Brain. Retrieved June 24, 2022, from https://www.parentingforbrain.com/how-to-be-a-good-parent-10-parenting-tips/

Lindberg, S. (2018, July 25). 12 tips for forgiving yourself. Healthline. Retrieved June 24, 2022, from https://www.healthline.com/health/how-to-forgive-yourself

Lyness, D. A. (Ed.). (2018, July). Your child's self-esteem (for parents) - nemours kidshealth. KidsHealth. Retrieved June 24, 2022, from https://kidshealth.org/en/parents/self-esteem.html

Mahtani, N. (2020, March 12). 10 ways to stop a spiral of negative thinking in its tracks in 5 minutes or less. Well+Good. Retrieved June 24, 2022, from https://www.wellandgood.com/how-to-stop-negative-thinking/

Meditation for parents. Headspace. (n.d.). Retrieved June 24, 2022, from https://www.headspace.com/meditation/parents

Mindful parenting. Child Mind Institute. (2021, October 12). Retrieved June 24, 2022, from https://childmind.org/article/mindful-parenting-2/

The Nemours Foundation. (n.d.). Nine steps to more effective parenting (for parents) - nemours kidshealth. KidsHealth. Retrieved June 24, 2022, from https://kid shealth.org/en/parents/nine-steps.html

O'Brien, M. (2022, April 26). 4 keys to overcoming negative thinking for good - Melli O'Brien. Mrs. Mindfulness. Retrieved June 24, 2022, from https://mrsmindfulness.com/the-four-keys-to-ov ercoming-negative-thinkingfor-good/

Taran, R. (n.d.). Retrieved June 24, 2022, from https://www.randytaran.com/blog/how-to-stop -negativity-in-its-tracks

Sinrich, J. (2020, May 9). 7 meditation apps for parents who just need a minute. Healthline. Retrieved June 24, 2022, from https://www.healthline.com/health/parent ing/best-meditation-apps-for-parents

Smith, J. (2020, October 23). Want a more confident child? here is how. The Independent. Retrieved June 24, 2022, from https://www.independent.co.uk/life-style/health-and-f amilies/psychologist-says-parents-should-18-things-raise -more-confident-child-a7453631.html?amp

Thompson, H. (n.d.). What are self-regulations skills? (and how to improve them). Indeed Career Guide. Re- trieved June 24, 2022, from https://www.indeed.com/c areer-advice/career-development/self-regulation-skills

What is mindful parenting? Headspace. (n.d.). Re- trieved June 24, 2022, from https://www.headspace.co m/mindfulness/mindful-parenting

Wong, D. (2021, November 18). 12 skills that good parents have (backed by science). Daniel Wong. Retrieved June 24, 2022, from https://www.daniel-wong.com/2018/01/08/good-parenting-skills/